SIGNAL GRACE

T. M. Yates

ISBN: 978-0-9892232-0-1 (pbk.)
ISBN: 978-0-9892232-3-2 (ebook)

2013 Gettysburg 150th Anniversary
First Edition Paperback

Edited by Tiffany Yates Martin, FoxPrint Editorial
Book Cover Design by Daniel Rembert
Interior Design & Layout by www.integrativeink.com

Published by Tiffany M. Yates
P.O. Box 554
Hartwood, VA 22471
www.tmyates.com

Printed in the United States of America

This true story is dedicated to four great men:

St. Patrick, for whom the shamrock was a symbol of God,

My father, for whom it was a symbol of love,

And to two generals from the American Civil War:

Winfield S. Hancock, Union,
who raised the shamrock high above his head, and

Lewis A. Armistead, Confederate,
his lifelong friend, who died looking at it.

TABLE OF CONTENTS

THE BATTLEFIELD AND THE GUARDS

In the early days of my family, before their hearts were broken, my mother and father liked to tell one story in particular about my childhood.

I was just a baby in a crib, looking up at colorful mobiles and trying to grab something.

"What is she trying to do?" my dad asked.

"Oh, my . . . look!" my mom replied. "It's the sunlight. She's trying to grab the light."

I saw the rays of sunlight as dust motes drifted through them, lighting up like fireflies in the bright realms. I grabbed at the sunbeams, trying to master the magic of these bright things. My parents watched as I flailed and grasped in my floundering attempts, entranced with the effort. To them, it was simple, sweet, and beautifully innocent in its futility. They knew sunbeams were not made to be caught.

Ever since I was a very small child, I wished that real magic existed in the world—not the wizardry of fairy tales, but a wonderful loving magic that came from God and made people happy. For a long time, my idea of magic prevented me from recognizing the power and mystery already present in the world and in the people I knew and loved. Instead I searched for signs, like one might find in a book: mysterious symbols, elaborate robes, and tiny unmarked jars of stardust.

Real magic doesn't work that way. Magic reveals itself to those who are humble enough and wise enough to look for it in the simple things. It is everywhere, but it is also well hidden. Seeing real magic requires a purification process of sorts, consisting of a lot of tears and time spent navigating the very dark, more unpleasant realms of one's own mind. The places where rotting bridges span large chasms over black, unfathomable waters.

Years later, in 2010, I stood thinking about this in a quiet battlefield cemetery in Fredericksburg, Virginia. Twilight descended on the soft green hillside, and the warm breeze tingled against my skin. It was Memorial Day weekend and the cemetery glittered, awash in a sea of fifteen thousand candles. As I watched the candlelight flicker on a tombstone, the grey stone a cold and quiet tribute, I thought about my dad and the spy.

The wind wafted gently over the graves of thousands of Civil War soldiers. I sighed deeply, breathing in and letting go. I thought I was at the end of the story, that everything was resolved and the loose ends, what were left of them, were slowly floating together into completion.

But I was wrong. It was all just beginning.

꿔

My father's name was Michael Weston Yates. The last name was standard Old English. In the massive riverbed of family names in the United States, it was a forgettable pebble. I remembered hearing a story about the name during the whirlwind of childhood: Hundreds of years ago, English lords, the rich men in a region, entrusted their most loyal servants to guard the gates and protect everyone. The English lords gave those guards a family crest and a last name that meant "the Gatekeeper." It was supposed to indicate someone who was loyal. Someone strong enough to stay awake . . . strong enough to guard during the long, dark hours of the night.

Michael Yates was a military man, a career officer in the United States Army, well built and slightly taller than average, with excellent posture that made him seem taller than he actually was. In fact, he stood so straight that he appeared to be overly dramatic, but he was just being himself. Thick eyeglasses defined the first impression of him and gave him a rather nerdy look, but his dark brown eyes were not the fearful eyes of an outcast. Powerful, they could flash fire or humor in a moment that could haunt the observer for years, and the purposeful way that he focused his energy hinted at an unusual and hidden strength.

My younger brother, Mark, and I both looked like him. We had large brown eyes and dark hair, although mine was very curly and Mark's was straight. We had his broad shoulders and tall body structure. Mark looked like a miniature of him. On the other hand, people often told me that I, through a certain turn of phrase or facial expression, more closely resembled our mother.

Our mother, Christine, was a refined woman. Her straight brown hair fell to her shoulders, and she took care to fix it beautifully each day for work. Her soulful eyes were a unique combination of green, blue, and grey. It was clear why my father had fallen in love with her. She was poised—graceful—and had a sharp eye for fashion. Liking the finer things in life but not often being able to afford them, she made the simplest things extraordinarily beautiful with a few creative adjustments. Of average height, she was beautiful and had an innate graciousness that suggested she was very well brought up. Her childhood, however, had been a catastrophe. Her father suffered a stroke when she was in high school; my mother worked full-time while attending school in order to keep the family going. The stress and isolation of that period affected much of what she did and how she approached life. She was a polite, thoughtful, and sweet woman who, when hurt by life's unexpected twists and less considerate participants, defaulted to a notion gained early on: The world was against her. When the going got tough (and it did), she dug trenches in her soul from which to fight. In some cases, the enemy appeared to be the majority of creation, but the fiercest, most destructive war she ever waged was with my father.

Our home was on a military post—Fort Meade, Maryland— among the hills and trees and, in winter, the snow. We lived in a modest house just off of the arterial road in the neighborhood, a street called 29th Division. The U.S. Army's 29th Division was inactive at the time, but famously symbolized the unity regained after the Civil War, drawing its members from Maryland in the North, as well as Virginia and North Carolina in the South. The division shoulder patches paid homage to the historical significance with a modified yin-yang design in blue and grey. But at the time, I didn't know any of that. Even my parents didn't care; they were too busy with the joys and challenges of new parenthood.

I was named after my dad. His name was Michael; my middle name was Michelle. When my mother was only sixteen years old, she knew several things beyond the shadow of a doubt: She would marry a man named Michael, have a daughter, and name that daughter Michelle after her father. Unfortunately, that truth didn't naturally make my father and me the best of friends. While I was growing up, we never managed to be close, as fathers and daughters are supposed to be. We didn't giggle together or share little jokes; we didn't really even see each other that often.

᭦

My memory is and always has been emotion-based. I remember being in the crib and reaching for those sunbeams: they were so beautiful. I felt attracted to them as if to my own long-forgotten soul. I wanted to be among them, to be a part of them, as if they were joy itself. I believed that we, the sunbeams and I, were of the same essence and I could know them. But they would not be held and soon faded, leaving only the colorful mobile and my parents' faces above my crib.

Conversely, I have a terrible memory when it comes to conflict. If there's a serious argument, just two minutes outside of it I often cannot recall what people said. Snapshots of the quarrel surface, like nasty little snippets, but I only accurately remember the underlying emotions. I have always thought that this lack of conflict memory was a great defect in me, that in order to make sense of the world and to speak aloud in it, I ought to be able to remember all of the viciousness along with the grandeur. But I can't do that. The memory slips away like a greased pig if I try to grasp it and, if I wrangle too desperately, morphs into an untrue thing. So I must describe, in some cases, the overarching perceptions, like an Impressionist painter illustrating war.

I cannot deliver a detailed version of what happened when my parents split. They divorced in 1985, when I was just three years old and Mark was a baby. Divorces are supposed to be between spouses, but like many things, it's not that simple. My father couldn't leave my mother and still be with us. To me, he just felt gone. The divorce didn't appear to be an amicable and cooperative thing. "Court"—I remembered hearing that word a lot. The separation of my mother and father seemed to be a hissing, spitting, fierce fight, after which it took time for the two combatants to retreat to their corners of the ring and for the dust to settle.

When things stabilized after a few months, Mark and I saw our dad off and on—twice in a lean year, ten times in a fatter one. Most of the time, visits with him were on major holidays like Thanksgiving or Christmas. Our father served in the military at various posts, and was constantly busy and very far away. He served his entire life with the U.S. Army, starting first in a combat capacity with the 82nd Airborne until a parachuting accident injured him and left him partially deaf in one ear. After that accident, most of his work was in nursing and clinical psychiatry. Mom, meanwhile, was very protective of us—although I didn't realize it at the time—and carried the remnants of our family forward in a determined way, insisting on routine and structure. Her gentleness and generosity disguised a core of iron. She actively tried not to say negative things about our father, and made it clear that she wanted the two of us children to have a good relationship with him. But she was bitter about the divorce, and the occasional choice comment slipped through her parenting filter.

My father had, apparently, fought her tooth and nail when it came to child support, and she believed that he lied in court about some issues. I don't know the details, but her resentment was fundamental to their interactions throughout the years. As generous and forgiving as she was, because of their difficulties my mom felt my dad to be dishonest and cheap, unwilling to inconvenience himself in any way, even for the welfare of his own children. And it made her ferociously angry. I was not immune to her perspective. In later years I saw that he *was* dishonest here and there—telling someone point-blank that he had put a check in the mail already (when I knew he hadn't even written it), or saying he had fulfilled other minor obligations when he absolutely hadn't. My father's dishonesty and my corresponding feeling of distrust made a huge impression on me, all the more so because he wasn't around much. I mentally distanced myself from him. Survival, after all, depended on my mom; I looked to her for everything.

"I'm really sorry how everything has worked out, Tiffany. I wanted to give you and Mark a life full of love and family. The stability I never had," she used to say to me. "But it's not really working out that way."

Because of her concern about the divorce and the effect it would have on us, when I was about four years old, she found some child psychologists who helped with the trauma of divorce on young children. Mark got to play in a room with colored blocks, while I was ushered into a dimly lit office. My mom assured me that the psychologist was a nice person, a friend I should talk to. After making sure that I understood how important this meeting was, she left the room so I could be counseled without the subtle influences of a parent's presence.

In retrospect, it wasn't the best plan.

I sat in a chair on one side of a small desk by myself while the psychologist, a young man, smiled at me from the other side. He opened up and chatted very nicely about silly things. *How is this going to help anything?* I thought. *What do I need help with?* But my mom had said that it was important. She had made it clear that we needed to support one another. So I sat there, well behaved and polite, and wondered when something important would happen. We talked about home and family for what seemed like a long time.

"Do you think your mom and dad will ever get back together?" the psychologist asked.

The truth was fierce within me. I wondered many times whether my parents would ever reunite, hoped that they would, and finally realized they wouldn't, but this was the first time I'd ever admitted it out loud: "Oh, no. Never!"

The psychologist leaned back, shocked—perhaps by the strength of my reply. *Did I do something wrong?* I looked for clues as to how I had failed so completely. He laughed.

"Well! That's an awfully strong answer! Never is a long time. Why never?"

But as he spoke, something in his face told me the truth: He was pretending. *He doesn't really care. I told him the truth and he laughed at me!*

Something in me shut down.

The psychologist saw that he had lost me. He tried to win back my trust by backing up and talking about other things. But I didn't want to talk anymore.

Afterward, there seemed to be a consensus that Mark and I were doing well enough, and the sessions were expensive. My mom never brought me back. I felt relieved; I didn't want to talk about my family ever again. I could do things better alone, just figuring it out by myself. I wanted a happy family, and my dreams were tender to the touch. I didn't want people laughing at them.

Never underestimate the willpower of a four-year-old. I forced myself into the steadiest place in my mind and, from there, taught myself to stop wishing. If I wanted my dad to be there, and he wasn't, I would be sad. I knew it would take more energy and strength to try again. I withered my hopes into compliance, deliberately imagining the disappointment and disaster that was sure to follow if I kept holding on.

❧

After the divorce, my dad sometimes appeared in my dreams, but in them he was not a nice guy. In a recurring nightmare, I stood alone in a doorway looking toward the front door of a house. I watched as my dad screamed at my mom in the living room, pushed her violently to the floor, and then tried to strangle her. Tiny and helpless, I didn't have enough strength to stop him and save her. The world was ending. Safety was just an illusion, a silky veil shredded without effort. There was no such thing as protection.

Dad is going to kill Mom.

And when he comes after me next, what will I do?

Waking up in the middle of that dream fight, I would open my eyes in my bedroom and lie curled up, terrified, under the comforter. Sometimes I grabbed a stuffed animal as quickly as possible, eventually burying myself under a pile of unicorns, horses, and a giant teddy bear until only one eye was peeking out at the world. Sometimes I imagined G.I. Joe and Rainbow Brite stood guard at the foot of my bed. (I didn't know what Rainbow Brite would do, but she had a lot of magic colors. Surely she could do something helpful to keep the monsters and meanies at bay.)

The fear slowly dissolved, but the distrust of my dad stayed.

In fact, it grew stronger.

I started referring to him as "Michael," not "Dad"—like my mom did. I never called him Michael to his face, though. Something told me he would not like that. Even then I felt the guilt and darkness of a mild cowardice, as if I betrayed him on a daily basis but changed face when he was around. But I was just trying to survive. When he was gone, I couldn't think of him as "Dad" because it hurt too much to miss him. I had to push him away in my mind. So he became, through the years and the distance, an outside entity. Mark and I lived separate lives from him, following like tiny foals in the shadow of our mom. On any given day, I was never quite sure where my dad was, or what he was doing.

WAR AND CHURCH

Michael was born and raised in the depths of southern Louisiana, among the wide and bent trees of the swamps. Cajun country. He grew up in the middle of the grimy city, attending Roman Catholic school every year until he graduated. He was the eldest of four siblings in a Catholic family. His mother was a half-Irish, half-Native American woman named Mary Burke who christened him in honor of an archangel. His father, Weston, was a Louisiana farm boy and an army veteran—a rough, unforgiving man who regularly beat his three sons. Due to some ambiguous circumstances, Weston did not believe Michael was his son for many years. My grandfather returned home from the Korean War and was particularly hard on my father growing up. However, Michael grew older and started to look like Weston. And Weston began to mellow around the same time Michael grew old enough to fight back.

The constraint and difficulties of those early years influenced a lot of Michael's behavior. Or perhaps it was innate self-discipline. He chose words carefully and did not curse. The closest I ever heard him come to cursing was exclaiming, "Ah, heck!" He didn't drink, smoke, or do drugs, and he exercised dutifully. His body was strong and lithe, and as a result he had many admirers. If he had an obvious vice, it was for sweets. He loved desserts and treats, often having chocolate-chip cookies for dinner.

Michael lived like a bachelor for two decades after the divorce, but my mother remarried quickly, just a year or so later. My new stepfather was a Methodist army chaplain named Randall who also happened to live on Fort Meade. An extraordinary preacher, he held congregations spellbound throughout sermons. Daily life in our new household had a lot of God. Randall and my mom practiced singing with the choir, prepared for sermons, and discussed prayers and theology. I can remember trips from one church to another, making it just in time for Randall to speak from another pulpit. I began to feel comfortable in churches, and my mom and Randall always encouraged me and Mark to see God as a friend—and to pray. It was a transitory existence; chaplains were shipped from church to church as needed. Somewhere along the line, in the small town of Veribest, Texas, I was baptized Methodist.

Michael wasn't around much. Since both he and Randall were in the military, home in any circumstance was subject to the whims of national interest. A map of their moves would look like the random, enthusiastic scribbles of a school-age child armed with two crayons, scrawling across the page of the country. But that artist was the U.S. Army, and those lines were our lives. The two rarely intersected. Michael did, however, occasionally visit; thus, I squeezed him awkwardly into my idea of family. He perched uncomfortably in my mind, like something that should fit but didn't: a cotton T-shirt that shrank, or a travel mug wobbling, a liquid threat in the center console. I wasn't quite sure what to do with him.

Sometimes I felt really sad for him—*he must be lonely*— and at other times I fancied that he must be doing very important things. But most of the time—when I remembered him—I just regretted that he and Mom didn't get along. I tucked uncomfortable feelings—like my quiet distrust of him—away as neatly as I could when he was around. I acted parts a lot, different ones depending on who was around, and pretended everything was normal. At the time, it was a very sincere kind of acting: I just wanted everybody to be happy. The problem was, when the other "actors" went to bed or left, I couldn't remember which face was mine, who "I" was, or how "I" felt.

When I was about six or seven years old, I started looking forward to visits with him. They were adventures. He always had things planned: new places to visit or people to meet. Something very different from our normal lives. But the visits were never long, so I did not sink into time with him like one would into an easy chair, safe and snug. I stayed a little aloof to protect myself, and my approach was justified each and every time: He always left.

Mark and I spent most of our days growing up with Randall and our mom. We lived in parsonages in Maryland, Texas, and Pennsylvania before finally moving to California, where we landed in Merced, a small city in the fertile Central Valley region. Like tiny teammates, we built forts, climbed trees, and rode bikes together in the parking lots by the churches. We Rollerbladed together in the neighborhood, staging races and playing with the other kids. Mark, in particular, loved model airplanes and boats. He also loved fire. He built model warships, sometimes spending weeks getting the details just right. Then, when he had one just perfect, he would light it on fire in a bucket of water, delighting in the destruction like a victorious admiral at sea. The water turned strange colors, and sometimes a horrible smell emanated from the wreckage. During times like that, he babbled excitedly about the *Bismarck* and *PT-109*. Every now and then he would screech, "Fire in the hole!"

When Michael visited, he thought Mark's bucket warships were a hilarious, amazing hobby. He diligently took us to hobby stores to get new ship models. Michael and Mark spent time picking out a wooden flagship with just the right number of cannons, or an aircraft carrier with the right number of planes. Sometimes Mark had to light the models a few times before they would sink, or before they were black enough that he considered the battle over. I didn't really get it. I did, however, evaluate the potential wrecks on the store shelves like a good sister, and watched the tiny warships burn with the objective curiosity of a scientist. I wanted to see which part burned first and why, and at what angle the ship finally sank to the bottom of the bucket . . . but in general I preferred horses.

Often our entire family stayed late into the evening at the churches; I played and hid in the dusty, unfrequented storage rooms, where statues of Mary and Jesus sat next to the large bells of the bell choir and the thick velvet drapes used to decorate for the holidays. I liked the quiet echoes of an empty church. Sometimes it seemed like God was really there. But I could feel Him only when I was by myself. Not in the crowds and the chatter.

When we saw our "real" dad, it was in short bursts—in Germany, Louisiana, and Texas—wherever he was stationed. When he was a captain stationed at Fort Bliss in El Paso, Texas, we watched sunsets and raced the sun in his red Jeep Cherokee. As we drove west on the highway with the windows down, the air streaming in and ruffling my hair, I felt like an unknown hero in the backseat, full of wonder and strength and glory—*who else on Earth has raced the* sun?! It was something from the pages of myths and titans! We were probably going about fifty miles per hour, and he had rolled the windows down for effect, but Mark and I were on board and having the time of our lives.

But on the whole, I wouldn't have known how to handle it if I actually had to talk to my father every day. There was, in fact, only one routine thing that happened with him, wherever we were at the time: He dragged me and Mark to the closest local Catholic church for Mass, or sometimes just to pray quietly and see the inside of the sanctuary.

Mass.

The big, dark, heavy word; that ponderous ritual consumed at least an hour of the day. Catholic Mass with Michael was very different from Methodist services with Randall. For one thing, the churches themselves were different. The Catholic churches, in general, felt serious and sad, as if grief had accumulated in the old spaces. Deep shadows in the sanctuaries, clusters of candles, and numerous saints made it seem to me like something, somewhere, had gone terribly wrong. If one were brokenhearted, they might have been harmonious and healing places; the ambience, oddly enough, suited my father perfectly. He kept his eyes focused toward the front, attuned to the altars and the priests. However, if you weren't grieving, as I was not, then it often felt as if someone were layering mounds of wet earth on your happy mood.

The Methodist churches with Randall, on the other hand, were sunnier and more cheerful. The Protestant trappings, straight broad lines of New World architecture, and large panels of color and wood in the sanctuaries were not places for sadness to linger. With Randall, Mark and I often arrived before anyone in the congregation so Randall could prepare; with Michael we dressed up (a little) and were almost always late. Michael chose a pew near the back and showed us when we were supposed to stand up and sit down. I didn't like it, being trapped in another dank, musty church listening to a deep voice drone on. Do right. Feel bad if you did wrong. I wriggled around in the pew and flipped through the pages of the hymnals and missals, feeling increasingly cramped and frustrated.

I tolerated Mass like a chore and my dad like an interesting specimen that might, just might, one day spurt forth an amazing piece of life-changing truth. Children want their parents to tell them real and important secrets, to let them in on the inner workings of the universe. That's why kids ask questions about even the blatantly obvious: an object, a person, the bright things hanging in a store window. I wanted the legend and the magic behind it all—and I believed Mom and Dad somehow knew the truth. Parents have the inside scoop on God and life. I watched him closely, but the miniature spans of life with him—those visits of days and weeks—didn't yield any secrets. He was just Dad, sometimes there and sometimes not.

As I grew older, I started to miss him when he wasn't around. Sometimes it was a mild, soft, and lonely feeling; at other times I sat, broken, in a little pile until the black sadness retreated. I wondered whether I'd somehow gone amiss. I did not know whether I was growing up the right way, if my inner self was straight with large, overarching branches, like the great majesty of plantation oaks, or if I grew warped and twisted, like the coastal trees between continents and oceans.

THE PRESIDIO

When I was nine, shortly after we moved to Merced, California, in 1991, my mom and Randall hit a rough patch. I didn't know exactly what went wrong, but I could see that they were breaking apart, like a ship against the rocks of a foreign shore. Mark and I hid in our rooms while they argued late into the evenings. Sometimes I would go into Mark's room to check on him, to make sure he was okay. Neither of us liked the yelling. Things would change again. I could feel it coming. The air tingled, as before a storm. Mom was angry, less flexible; I wasn't sure why. But I knew Randall would leave and someone else would come in—just like what happened with Michael.

While we were in Merced, the army transferred Michael to the Presidio of San Francisco on the coast of California. His move there marked the first time in years that he had been relatively close to us; now he was less than two hours away. *Presidio* means "fort" in Spanish, and the Presidio of San Francisco was, at the time, an army post that occupied some of the most desirable property in the entire United States. Once a strategic military location, the San Francisco Peninsula now served the nation as an altar primarily to commerce and finance, decorated with skyscrapers and tourist attractions in the form of the city of San Francisco, which sat at the northern end. The Presidio crowned the uppermost tip of the San Francisco Peninsula, anchoring the famed Golden Gate Bridge.

The army couldn't have made Michael happier with a transfer to anywhere else in the world, because it was so close to us. After he settled in, in December of 1991, he brought us to the Presidio to

show us around his new home, admiring our luck all the while—
that we now lived close to one another; that we had such a nice
home on the Presidio; that we were even now together.

Talk of the impending split between Randall and our mom
surfaced. I don't remember how or why; this update was in fact a
rather routine one in the course of trips, visits, and absences. Both
Michael and our mom possessed mildly toxic curiosity about each
other, and Mark and I satisfied their interest. We shared information between houses like tiny strategists, although I didn't realize it
at the time. I can't speak for Mark, but I, at least, delighted in these
moments of influence, where we (the kids) could actually inform
them (the parents). One of them would inquire of the other's activities or life in manners that ranged from overly casual to outright
direct. It felt to me, always, like maneuvering. However, there were
moments when either Mom or Michael would look almost vulnerable while questioning us, as if their hearts were suddenly unveiled
like a long-awaited sculpture.

And that broke my heart. *They hurt!*

Sometimes I could sense when the topics—bedtime, dinners—
were a stick of dynamite that might explode. Michael especially
appeared awkward sometimes, guarded and uncertain in his choice
of words, as if he might do the wrong thing with regard to me and
Mark and provoke my mom's wrath. Strangely enough, I despised
him for that clumsiness; I thought it was cowardly. *He should do
what he thinks is right, regardless of anyone else!* But part of me also
understood: my mom's anger, while rarely intense, was ferocious
when it related to us—and a low-level constant as it related to him.
He clearly did not want to not heighten that sea state.

Updates in our conversation this time around included Randall
moving out. Michael never ventured past a certain point when it
came to Mom's romantic interests. At such junctures, he would
redirect the conversation skillfully. This time, he looked out the
Jeep's front windshield: "San Francisco is amazing. Tiffany, Mark,
you two will love the Presidio. There's so much to do; there's so
much history!"

Michael often said a person's name as he was talking to him or
her, almost as if honoring or validating their presence, and far from

being an awkward interjection, it tended to anchor or recall the listener to the moment and the topic at hand. It was an odd habit but, as it had positive effects, people (including us) tended to adjust to his manner of speaking. Michael chauffeured us over the Bay Bridge past Treasure Island, up and down the unusually steep city streets, past terraced blocks, all the while talking about the city and its landmarks. A spirit of curiosity pervaded the Jeep as it chugged along in the invigorating chill of the bay breezes.

He was a history enthusiast, always somehow digging up tiny, obscure pieces of local lore. Even after just a week somewhere, he could offer a tour like a professional guide. We drove a scenic route, an extremely circuitous path that, in many cases, took us in exactly the opposite direction of our destination. He described different cities throughout the world, illuminating by contrast and example how special San Francisco was: "Here in San Francisco you have the bay, and if you want to do something, all you have to do is walk out your door. Somewhere, something cool is happening: Just look at those windsurfers!"

Mark and I gawked, neither of us having seen windsurfers before; they were like colorful guitar picks dancing erratically in the water, and every now and then, one of them would fall flat in an ignoble flop, temporarily defeated in the bout with Mother Nature. Finally, we arrived at the Presidio's Lombard Gate. The entrance was situated near Letterman Hospital, where my dad now worked now as a major, doing something related to psychiatry (although I didn't understand exactly what). He then took us on a first-class tour of the Presidio grounds, pointing out the stately parade field and historic buildings of the old fort, all surrounded by the huge eucalyptus trees that cover the northernmost tip of the bay's peninsula. On the way to his new home, he drove us by Crissy Field near the water and then the San Francisco National Cemetery. Passing the gravestones from a distance, he commented, "A spy from the Civil War is buried in there. I've wanted to check that out. Would you two like to go?"

"Oh, yeah! What did he do?" Mark asked.

"I don't know."

"Where is it? Can you see the grave from the street we're on?" I asked.

"I'm not sure. We don't have time right now, but we'll go together the next time y'all are up here," our dad said. "That would be a very cool thing to do."

Mark and I perked up. The resting place of a secret agent! Surely a master of espionage would have an awesome monument. As we passed the huge stone gates of the lonely cemetery, we searched for the spy's memorial among the tombstones nestled in the hillside. The brief glimpse inside offered nothing—only an impression of the place. There was no movement. Just clean rows and green grass. A reminder that things end.

Michael drove on, and I twisted my head this way and that to catch a view of everything the adventurer in the driver's seat pointed out.

"You guys have got to check out this turn up ahead. The first time I took it, I thought the Jeep was going to tip over!"

We went up, and the car keeled far to the side as the road lurched upward, as if the Earth were a bronco unwilling to be ridden. The Jeep rocked, a common occurrence on the hills of San Francisco, and Michael got the chorus he wanted from the backseat:

"Whoa, that was awesome!"

"Can we do it again?"

We finally arrived at his small apartment. It was a simple base housing unit in a cluster of several unassuming brown buildings nestled among towering eucalyptus trees. Outdoors, the air was cool and forever fragrant, permeated with the smell of the trees and the sea. Inside was a different story. The apartment was a little musty, its ambiance slightly better than that of a storage unit. As usual in his temporary homes, there was not much in the way of decoration. The walls were bare. Each piece of furniture was awkwardly displayed in the center of the room. The entire place was a shelter, not a home. Creature comforts being in short supply, it was merely a base for exploring, deeply unsatisfying if one preferred a cozier, more comfortable style of living.

When he first showed us the apartment, Michael was almost apologetic that it was so small. He described where stuff was and then waited quietly, eyes eager and alert, for our reaction. We both sensed his anticipation. We actively complimented features and the placement of furnishings—as guests might in a new acquaintance's house for the first time—and found reasons to openly admire the new place. Even kids can sense when someone needs a little reassurance.

His apartment boasted a tiny kitchen, which he'd stocked with supermarket brands of parenting convenience—Chef Boyardee and Dinty Moore beef stew—supplemented by cookies and some miscellaneous cans of peas and corn. He tended to lump various vegetables on our plates with the perfunctory, uninterested *kerplunk* of fatherly duty. Even he didn't seem to enjoy them. That evening, he ladled out some macaroni and cheese along with a piece of chicken on three plates and set our dinners on the place mats in front of us. There was a weighty pause as something struck him about our meal. He scrunched his face and observed, unsatisfied, "Hmm. Everything's yellow."

Mark and I looked down at our plates. It was true. I admired the different shades. Michael, however, was disappointed with the nutritional value of a limited palette and announced, "We need something green."

He sought out a can of peas. Warming them delayed our dinner a few moments, but it was soon time for the prayer, which Michael led: "We are thankful for our food, for our friends, and family too. Before we eat we say 'thank you.' Amen."

We all sat back down, with Michael much more relaxed, as if he had done his duty now that two colors were on the table. While we ate, he shared a poem: "I eat my peas with honey. I've done it all my life. It may taste kind of funny, but it keeps them on the knife."

We cajoled him immediately and he laughed, relenting. He got the honey out so each of us could try, with varying degrees of success, to eat peas with a knife. It tasted awful, as one might suspect, and the peas were prone to running away like kindergarteners at recess. But it was fun.

Past the kitchen in the small living room, he had a sparse arrangement of furniture, which happened to be the same actual furnishings—either by accident or sentimental intention—that he owned when he was married to our mom. He'd sworn, when he divorced my mom, that he would never marry again. I think I initially heard that from my mom, but Michael confirmed it several times over the years. He told me once it was because he was Catholic, but I didn't believe him. Sometimes he said things I knew weren't true; I sensed they were just white lies for convenience, to make somebody feel better, or to avoid trouble. I didn't know enough about Catholicism to argue either way, but watching what he did and hearing what he said, I believed it was because he suffered somewhere deep inside. There was a discontent and sad fatigue within him, as if he had been gingerly crouching in a dark place for years, all while telling people he was fine. It hurt me to see that. I didn't know about love then and I didn't fathom his heart. But I could see that he and life—parts of it, at least—were not very good friends. At any rate, he certainly seemed to live that declaration, some part of him frozen in the past, with her.

A GIFT

There was only one new piece of furniture in Michael's apartment: a tall bookshelf holding a meager selection of books. He must have been reading those books recently: He only unpacked absolute necessities, and had entire boxes that hadn't been opened in years. A room dedicated to boxes, unceremoniously dubbed "the Box Room," had been around for as long as I could remember in every place he ever lived. Anything visible in his house was either necessary to existence or else very current to his life right then. Most of these books related to military history: espionage, famous conflicts, and renowned generals. One book in particular caught Mark's attention and mine:

The Killer Angels.

The title confused me. *How can you be a killer and an angel?* I wondered. I wanted to read the book just so the title would make sense, so those two words would not be sitting in my mind and grating at me. Mark picked the book up and I peered over his shoulder. A battle scene covered the front and back covers. On the front, a rider twisted precariously on a white horse. Mark handed the book to me and I examined it more closely: a horse down, wounded men.

"Hey, Dad, have you read this book?" I asked.

"Which one?"

"*The Killer Angels.*"

He entered the living room as the sun came through the patio door and fell on the rough fabric of the lonely brown couch from the 1970s. "Oh, yes. *The Killer Angels* is about the Battle of Gettysburg, which was a turning point in the Civil War. It's very good. If either of you want to read it, I think you would enjoy it. They made a movie about that book a few years ago."

He departed into the kitchen and came back a second later. Something else had clearly occurred to him.

"*Bury My Heart at Wounded Knee* is very good too," he added.

He disappeared again.

I picked up the two books and reviewed the front and back covers of both. I wasn't very interested in *Bury My Heart at Wounded Knee* (it just looked sad), but *The Killer Angels* sounded mysterious and exciting. If Michael thought it was good, it probably was. I wondered why he liked it. Michael read books in a weird way: He always read the name of the publisher, the publication date, and the name of the author out loud before starting the book itself. Those small facts seemed to anchor, through a tiny act of ritual, the reality of the book and its message in his mind. He was an encyclopedia of any book that he had ever read; years after reading one he could remember when it was published.

A few minutes later, Michael asked from the kitchen, "Do you guys want to go on a hike?"

"Where?" we both asked.

"There's a great trail I found really close by."

We went. Just down the road from his apartment was a breathtaking view of the Pacific Ocean, the spectacular result of the high hill and a break in the wall of tall coastal trees. Michael called it Lookout Point, although apparently it had some other official name that I never knew. He entered one of the trailheads near the road and hiked confidently down the hillside, deep into the bramble and brush, a lot farther than I thought anyone ought to go. I followed, trying to avoid contact with the brambles whenever possible. Normally a tomboy, playing soccer and wrestling in the grass with glee, I became, with strange plants on a narrow trail, a fastidious little princess in hiking boots. Full of irrational concerns, I worried incessantly. Could we get in trouble for trespassing? Whose land was this? And then, a darting black movement a few feet from my shoe: Oh, my God, was that a *mouse*?!

Michael looked back at me, amused. I made my way down the hillside deliberately, slowly gaining confidence that creatures with large teeth weren't hiding in the bushes and that it was okay that we were hiking on this hill, until I finally relaxed and trotted forward, able to enjoy the sunset and the Marin headlands. By the time we got to the lower roadway, a street that split the hillside in two, with the upper brambly slope and a lower sandy one, our faces were flushed and we were all smiling. Mark and I begged Michael to take us across the road and go down the lower slope, or, if he wouldn't take us, to at least let us go over and look. He evaluated the darkening sky and said, "It's too late. Maybe next time. That would be fun! We can do that next time you guys come up to the Presidio."

As soon as he said that, I boxed away my hopes for the lower slope. It would be a long time before we got to hike down that.

🦇

We returned to our mom's house the following morning, and slipped back into the homely triad of school, playing outside, and growing up. Despite the fact that Michael was relatively close now, we weren't able to see him often. He was busy with work, and I remember him visiting about once a month. Even then, sometimes he would drive into the Central Valley and stay there, rather than take us back to the Presidio. When he stayed in the valley, if the weather was nice he would take me and Mark to go play catch with a football at Bear Creek Park in Merced. He loved that city park and its large trees. I hated it when he drove away.

Once, for some logistical reason, our mom was also in the Jeep with us on the way home from the park. It was one of those uncommon occasions—like once a decade—when all four of us were in the same vehicle together. The windows were rolled down. The fresh California air breezed by, carrying all the twilight sounds of songbirds and crickets. Mom and Michael didn't hate each other; we were all happy and driving together! I beamed in the backseat. All was right with the world. When Michael parked in front of our house, Mark and I begged him to drive around the block just once more time. We wanted a couple more minutes together. He did, and I basked in the rare sense of completeness, but even as he drove I knew it could never be long enough.

❧

A few weeks later, on our next visit to the Presidio, I picked up *The Killer Angels* first thing. Settling comfortably into the corner cushions of the couch, I began to read. The pages were a little rough; my fingers, as they found the next page and slid down, made a soft sound like a woodworker sanding. I don't know why that sound stuck out to me. I didn't mind; it became an unconscious rhythm, the music behind our getting to know each other—this author and me.

When Michael dropped us back off at our mom's house at the end of the weekend, I clambered out of his Jeep clutching *The Killer Angels*. I hadn't quite finished and had asked him whether I could borrow it—I didn't want to wait until we saw him again to know how it ended. He eagerly let me have it; he encouraged curiosity and reading with religious zeal. From the first introduction of the commanding generals, lined up in the chaos and glory of their lives, to the quiet, rainy conclusion, I was mesmerized. The book consumed me; the Civil War was all I thought about for weeks afterward. I wanted to know more about all of these people who came alive on the pages of Michael Shaara's world. History suddenly felt like something real. (I also had a mild crush on General Longstreet.) When I left the real world and its concerns, disappearing into the book, I could feel the heat of the July day, as if I were walking through the dust, my eyes squinting in the pervasive summer sunshine of Pennsylvania. I could hear the horses neighing and see the power of their bodies, their legs, as they dashed and trampled across the fields. I could hear the sounds of violent combat getting closer.

THE SPY

A few months after our first visit to the Presidio, we ventured to the National Cemetery to see the grave of the Civil War spy. Michael had not been yet either, so we all had to hunt for it. There was, in the center of the cemetery, a large broad loop called the Circle of Honor, and the spy's grave was in that circle. Michael carried a cemetery brochure and read aloud the spy's aisle and grave number. We counted the aisles up to the right one, and then the tombstones inward to the center of the circle. Suddenly we stood right in front of it.

There were no elaborate decorations; it could hardly have been a simpler tombstone. It read:

PAULINE C. FRYER
UNION SPY

Oh, my! I thought. *It's a girl!*

"What did she do? Do you think she was afraid?" I asked, hoping for a compelling story.

"Oh, gosh, yes," Michael responded. "I don't think anyone could be in circumstances like that and not be afraid. I don't know much about her, but I know she was a somewhat famous actress. Her acting skills probably came in handy while she was behind enemy lines." He turned around and pointed. "There are also some Congressional Medal of Honor winners nearby."

As we drove away, I looked at the passing stones and shifting views of the green grass and thought, *Soldiers. Spies. There's a lot of courage in that circle.*

The red Jeep clattered on and I peered out the window. *Behind enemy lines.* That did sound dangerous. I thought for all I knew of him, Dad could be a spy. I looked at the back of his head, his dark hair as he drove. I imagined him behind enemy lines. He was strong. He was in great shape physically, and there was something about his spirit that told me that if he ever set his mind to something serious, he wouldn't stop until it was done—or until he was dead. His spirit was so tough in that regard that, as I contemplated the possibility that he might be a spy, I only felt bad for the enemy.

❧

Starting with *The Killer Angels* and Pauline Fryer, my interest in the Civil War became insatiable. I started researching, piecemeal, famous figures and different battles. I liked the personal stories best. Friendships. Famous letters. The story of generals Lewis Armistead and Winfield Scott Hancock fascinated me: Armistead and Hancock served in the U.S. Army together and became great friends; they fought together in the Mexican-American War. But when the Civil War started, Armistead went to the Confederacy, while Hancock remained with the Union, both men thinking they were doing the most honorable thing they could under the circumstances.

According to a combination of legend and history, before the Civil War really gained momentum there was a party in Los Angeles, California, that several future Union and Confederate senior commanders attended. Armistead and Hancock were among them. At that party, Armistead, a man of strong passions, both loyal and flawed, gave Hancock's wife his personal prayer book, inscribed with the words, *Trust in God and fear nothing.*

He then told Hancock, "Good-bye; you can never know what this has cost me."

To my way of thinking at the time, all that California had in the way of history was the Gold Rush and a haphazard line of

Spanish-Catholic missions dangling on its coastline like a string of Christmas lights. The East Coast crackled with history; I wanted to immerse myself in it. The people who lived on the East Coast were lucky to be so close to places where powerful people transformed the world. It would be so cool to live by Gettysburg! I thought. I wanted to visit those battlefields someday.

⤳

Mark was also interested in military history; because of our mutual curiosity, our mom bought the movie *Gettysburg* for the three of us to see together. All of us loved the film; it stayed very true to the actual book. In fact, it ended up being one of our favorite movies.

Soon thereafter, Mark and I visited Michael at the Presidio again for Memorial Day weekend. Memorial Day was very important to Michael. He insisted every year on celebrating in a special way, even if it just meant watching a ceremony or driving by a monument. The army scheduled a large ceremony to honor fallen veterans that day; it was to be held at the San Francisco National Cemetery.

An army general spoke in front of a large semicircle of colored wreaths, each one donated by a military unit or civilian social club and dedicated to veterans and particular military units. After the ceremony, Michael brought us to the stage to see the massive wreaths up close. One, a large white wreath with stargazer lilies in the center, caught Michael's attention.

"Oh, wow, this one was made to honor the Union soldiers who died in the Civil War. Let's take this wreath to Fryer's grave!"

Immediately aghast that he even suggested the idea, Mark and I were reluctant. It felt like stealing. I worried that Michael might get in trouble; besides, wouldn't it look a little silly to be carrying a huge wreath across a cemetery, *away* from the public ceremony? "Can we do that? Doesn't it belong to somebody?"

"Well, yeah," Michael replied, "but the ceremony's done. Let me check." He walked away to talk with an event official. Securing permission—which not only surprised me but allayed my fears about his arrest—he hoisted the huge wreath with ease and carried it to Fryer's tombstone. Mark helped him rest the wreath against her name.

"Now for pictures!" Michael exclaimed.

We posed, each in turn, at the grave with the wreath. Then Mark took a picture of Michael, who, for his turn, hunched low next to the wreath. He smiled broadly and appeared as excited as if he were posing with a living celebrity. Neither Mark nor I understood why Fryer was so important to Michael. But there was something mysterious and peculiar—almost momentous—about being there with him.

Michael Yates did not like to forget. He did not seem to like any slippage, even of minor things, into the abyss of memory.

꙰

Early the following year, when I was in fifth grade, in the intervening weeks between a couple of his visits, I found a "Best Friends" necklace set at a local store. It was a small circle, split in two so that two friends could share the pieces and together make the complete set. I gripped the necklace set in my hand, and an idea captivated me.

Ever since we moved to California, colors, symbols, and codes had fascinated me. Ankhs, runes, peace signs, as well as practical communication codes that were unfamiliar to many people, including the NATO phonetic alphabet (military words for letters; e.g., alpha, bravo, Charlie . . .) and nautical flags held me spellbound. I don't remember noticing symbols before we moved there, or maybe I was just now old enough to notice them, but now I saw that California was bursting with ancient symbols all over the place—on everything from bumper stickers to monuments. I wondered why they were created, what they symbolized, and believed that the people who understood them must be very powerful.

I wanted to be conversant in all of them, to tell my friends what message was lifted above the water in a string of nautical flags, or to talk in pig latin; essentially, to understand everything I could about the world around me. An unexpected corollary of this fascination was that I eagerly wandered costume jewelry stores like Claire's, searching for these kinds of signs. I knew all of the merchandise was just flimsy trinkets, but I remained convinced that they must hold secrets, possess some powerful meaning, or be able to conjure transformative goodness. From animal designs, like spirit totems, to charm bracelets with miniature pianos and baseball bats, the collections enthralled me. It seemed as if these widely known symbols were almost like codes that could, in endless combinations, be made to reveal the mystic secrets of every person on Earth.

I looked down at the necklaces I clutched. The antiqued finish made them seem old and special. The set was perfect. My idea made me smile: I would buy it . . . but instead of giving half to a friend at school, like most of my classmates would have, I would give it to my dad. I was a little lonely at school sometimes. Even though I had friends, I didn't connect with them completely. I wondered whether Michael felt the same way in his life. He was by himself when he came to see us—and alone again when he left. I saw how my mom pushed him away from us, and it grated against my nature. I wanted everyone to be happy allies. He was the most achingly alone person I knew. I didn't really feel like his "best friend," but liked the idea of our sharing something.

The next time Michael came to visit, instead of all of us driving back to the Presidio, he remained in the Central Valley. We stayed at Castle Air Force Base, a military base close to our mom's house in Merced. Castle had a Blackbird airplane on display, along with something called a "Flying Fortress." When Michael first mentioned the Flying Fortress I imagined a castle (complete with turrets and a drawbridge) that could fly. But it was, disappointingly, just a World War II bomber. Mark and Michael spent a half hour wandering around it and discussing its possibly being haunted. I peeked into the windows to see if I could see any ghosts, but didn't notice any odd movements or misty vapors. I preferred the futuristic SR-71 Blackbird on display, a fearsome black plane that reminded me of a prowling panther. Now, that plane, I had no doubt, could get stuff done!

That evening, we stayed at the bachelor officers' quarters (BOQ)—which sounds like permanent housing but was actually a hotel—on the base. While we ate powdered doughnuts and watched a movie together in our hotel room, I decided now was the time. I went around to the side of the sofa and, unzipping my backpack, announced, "I have a present for you, Dad!"

He was sitting on the floor next to Mark and looked over his shoulder to me, his eyebrows suddenly raised. "Honey, you don't have to give me anything! I just love it when we're together!"

He seemed to mean it, but everybody likes presents, I reasoned. "I saw this and wanted to give half to you." I held up the necklaces.

Michael squinted, then patted Mark, stood up stiffly, and came over. I could smell his aftershave as he leaned over to see the pendants. I handed him the two necklaces so he could see them nestled in their display. He put his glasses on his forehead and, peering at the pendants a few inches from his face, read the tiny engraving.

His eyes widened (a little too much) and he exclaimed, "Oh, Tiffany! This is so sweet!"

He complimented it profusely, but my heart sank. He gamely put on a show of gratitude and enthusiasm because he thought it was important to me. I wanted him to think of me as an equal, to confide in and trust me. But he was treating me like a kid!

"This is just the best present!" he continued, giving me repeated hugs while Mark watched and grinned from his little perch on the other end of the sofa. Michael's hugs only served to reinforce the distance I felt between us. I recoiled, afraid I'd done something naïve and silly, but I tried to muster my original enthusiasm as I took the necklaces back from him and extracted them from their little display. I gave Michael the first half, the pendant that read, "BE / FRI." But I only glanced at him and smiled—so he'd feel comfortable. I realized I'd never be what I wanted to be to him—never be his true and genuine friend. He sometimes said I was important to him, but it I believed it was only in a small or ornamental kind of way. I felt the opposite of important. He wouldn't call me up and tell me what he thought about things, or ask me to join him in matters of consequence, in anything he really wanted to do. He wouldn't call me up if he needed help.

The next day, after he dropped us off at our mom's house, I spent time alone in my room. I berated myself for exposing my heart in a stupid and childish way. I hid my half of the necklace away in a treasure box so I wouldn't be reminded of my shame and then knelt nearby, shoulders hunched, just staring.

GUY

For whatever strange psychological reason, I constantly strained myself to help my mom maintain an even keel. She tended to have ups and downs, like anyone might, but sometimes if she was in a bad mood—mad or sad—it didn't go away easily. And she had been awfully tense and upset lately. I gathered there were serious problems surrounding basic issues, like finances, but she wouldn't confide in me. I was her daughter, and she acted as though it was her responsibility to protect me from difficulties.

I disagreed. Keeping the problems secret, locked tight in the vault of her mind, stressed her even more. And they inevitably boiled over. The unpleasant steam from the fires of her motherly worries, whatever they were, whistled out in hot rebukes, a constant feeling of unease, and one time an undeserved slap across the face before school. I wished she would just tell me what the deal was.

Soon after my mom and Randall split in the early 1990s, my mom started dating a man named Guy whom she'd met at work. I breathed easier when Guy was with us. He calmed her down better than I could. He was older and understood more than I did. He provided both stability and humor—and eased my burden of trying to anticipate her reactions.

"Hey, Tiff," he said one day about a year after he and my mom started dating, approaching me as I sat in the living room of our house in Merced, "why don't you come outside on the porch for a moment? I'd like to talk to you about something."

I hauled myself off the warm carpet in the living room where I'd been reading and followed Guy through the front door to the porch. I knew right away what it was about. Mark was off at a soccer game; I wondered whether I'd be the one to tell him the news when he returned.

Guy established himself on the swing as though it were a throne of sorts. There was nothing contrived in his posture; he tended to "own" wherever he was. I rather admired the way he sat; however, this time he suddenly appeared slightly unsure, off balance. He patted the spot next to him. I sat.

"You know I love your mom a lot, right?"

"Yes."

"Well . . ." This type of conversation was clearly not his thing. "What would you think if she and I got married?"

I loved my mom and liked Guy, but I had seen enough of couples to know that they didn't last. My mom's relationship with Michael, the great barometer of relationships to me, had been blasted to smithereens. That schism, along with the divorce from Randall and all of the silly little dating games that I saw happen at school—classmates dating for a few days, then some variation of minor drama and they were bitter enemies, until the next month— struck me as stupid, unnecessary friction. In my opinion, relationships were messy affairs.

Sitting with Guy on the porch, I could tell that this marriage idea wouldn't last either. *It would be nice if it did.* But I could see the future as if I had written it. So I regarded him, leaned forward, and tried to be as tactful as possible, ever the actor striving for harmony: "Are you sure you really want to do that?"

He burst out laughing.

"Oh, God," he said through the belly laughs, "I was expecting you to say all kinds of things, but I was not expecting *that!*"

He laughed for a while, started to recover, then looked at me and started chuckling again. I grinned, but I didn't get the joke. I giggled because his belly laughs were shaking the swing and knocking the rhythm off.

"Listen, Tiff," he said, recovering, "relationships are all about what you put into them. I love your mom and we believe this can work. So we're going to get married."

"Okay."

"And you guys will be moving up to my house in Modesto."

"Okay." I smiled. "That's cool. I like your house."

Modesto was bigger than Merced and had a different tempo, more suburban and less agricultural. Guy's house was big, clean, and within walking distance to a nice soccer field. I knew my mom, Mark, and I could make it anywhere—and now there was the prospect of having Guy around.

On June 29, 1995, my mom and Guy got married. I was thirteen years old.

I admired Guy. I admired his approach to life. My dad could be quirky and private at times. Guy did not seem like such a stranger. He was charismatic, communicative, and hilariously funny. Even when he was mistaken, he had buoyant confidence and intense resolve. And moreover, he told the truth. Because of that, he became a confidant. I referred to Michael, Randall, and Guy as "my three dads," but when there was a serious problem I went straight to Guy for advice. My dad remained lumped into the outer world—a figure against which one would occasionally likely need to defend.

A FIRE IN THE HEART

By the end of 1995, Michael was gone again.

The U.S. Army transferred him to Fort Polk, Louisiana. Before he left California, he sent me a Bible. He included a special note in that package: *This is a Catholic Bible, so there are some differences in text from other Bibles you may read. Don't let the differences get in the way of the Key Message of God's Love for Us.*

And with that, our time with our father in San Francisco was a memory.

He remained in Louisiana for a year and then deployed to Bosnia as part of a group that was to help control or minimize combat stress. While he was gone, first in Louisiana and then Bosnia, I finished junior high and entered high school. I lived in Modesto with my mom, Mark, and Guy in Guy's house in a quiet neighborhood behind Beyer, the high school I now attended. There are hundreds of small towns in the United States smaller than Beyer High School—it was huge. It dominated the surrounding parks, commercial properties, and residential neighborhoods. My life as a high school freshman was perfectly suburban: manicured and mundane. In class, I read about people who believed in what they did, who poured their hearts and lives into the causes they loved. I wanted to live like that. But no raging, fearsome, glorious call to meaning moved me. I wandered the halls of school a little confused about more fundamental things than calculus or history, wondering what I was supposed to do with my life.

When Mark and I were with my father in person, Michael bent over backward to help us have a good time together. Granted, our wants and needs weren't excessive—lunch at Wendy's, maybe—but there was, when we were with him, an expansive sense of abundance and consideration. It was as if he were permanently bent over looking at us, making sure we were okay and happy. However, when we apart, we almost fell off of his radar in the way of consideration and sweet gestures.

His letters, when he was in the States, were very short: often just a page with a couple of jokes. I actually liked when he was overseas in Bosnia, because I got heavier, more satisfying mail. His letters from 1997, while he was abroad, were longer. He described the reasons that Serbs, Croats, and Muslims didn't get along in the area, and sometimes included samples of foreign currency or photos. The photos were normally of the locals—one guy was roasting a pig—but there was one extraordinarily beautiful picture among the few he sent. He took it from a military vehicle as it drove down a roadway. The land and structures all around were burnt ruins, but the sky above was magnificent—huge clouds and horizons that stretched on forever.

The other trend I observed around that time related to his almost schizophrenic expressions of generosity and attentiveness toward us. He missed the holidays with us that year and said he really regretted it. As a surprise, he sent us a duffel bag full of presents. He had locked the huge black bag closed by drawing the two zipper pulls together in the middle and then putting a padlock through the eyelets. But aside from the letters and the duffel bag, I couldn't find satisfying representations of the same thoughtfulness he conveyed in person. I don't know what I was expecting or looking for, but whatever it was, I noticed the lack. It seemed as if he had turned his back. The shift from one way to the other was confusing, and I struggled to figure it out, trying to comprehend what was appropriate with regard to him.

I wondered a lot about him and where he had been. When Mark and I used to play in the Box Room, we discovered that Michael had been to many different cities—including Rome and Paris. I was shocked when I found notes outlining intense, detailed itineraries to see the Louvre and the Coliseum among many other sights. I thought of him as well-traveled and worldly, but he had never, that I remembered, mentioned Paris or Rome to me. These notes and ticket stubs, to me, were his treasures. He had obviously put a lot of time and thought into the visits, and tried so hard to see everything! As I sat there holding the old tickets in my hand, I remembered wishing that he had told us about the trips.

When I was fifteen, toward the end of my freshman year, Michael returned to the States—this time to San Antonio. This move was to be his last with the U.S. Army; he was going to retire. He had always said that he wanted to retire in San Antonio. He loved the Riverwalk and called the city "peaceful."

Since we were still apart, Michael tried to parent from afar with occasional handwritten notes and updates. Even though the messages of this period were just of the brief stateside variety, his letters and cards were fun to get, but they often arrived with all of fanfare of a visit to the supermarket: *Hey, a letter from Dad—cool, okay, time to go play.* "Please study hard in school and try to do the right things." In a card, he told us he'd purchased a house on street called Allensworth in San Antonio. In a different note, he wished me a happy sixteenth birthday, saying, *It's really quiet around San Antonio since you're not here. I can't wait til you + Mark come to visit. Love You Forever, Dad.*

None of us knew it then, but he was about to get quite the "visit."

❧

When I was in high school, I craved encouragement and camaraderie. My mom and Mark were very close; I sometimes felt like the third wheel in the family nucleus of our little trio. Guy was around, of course; however, as our mom's spouses came and went, my idea of "family" included three permanents and one temporary. Mom and Mark teased me incessantly about anything and everything—my jokes, my tendency to read alone in my room while everybody else laughed together, or whatever else they noticed as singular to me. The teasing was good-natured, but it was frequent and didn't encourage openness. I learned to either banter back playfully or ignore their jests, but it never seemed natural to me. I merely met them on the field they chose.

I had, not long after we moved to Modesto, been invited to participate in an exclusive soccer league in the area called Ajax. Modesto had a large recreational soccer association; this league was supposed to be especially competitive. I had been naturally athletic all of my life, but I was not innately aggressive. I strove instead for gentle harmony.

I was flattered that Ajax was interested in me, and it seemed, within the context of opportunities in Modesto, to be a good gig. Competitive athletes had virtually indestructible auras around high school and received positive attention from the community. The main reason I considered joining, though, was because my mom and Mark were so impressed. The playful taunts turned into compliments—and that felt great.

I joined.

From the very first practice it was evident that my new teammates were cliquish and vicious. I was a decent player, but far from the best. Any mistake made was a black smear, in the team opinion, to be redeemed only with repeated fantastic plays and compulsive allegiance to the team. With practices twice a week, there was no avoiding the pressure and negativity. I was just good enough to be slightly above pathetic on that team, and occasionally there would be rare successes, but they were few and far between, and my self-esteem corroded quickly.

I started to withdraw a bit, and my appearance might have suggested it. A tall girl, I had long, intensely curly hair that could be recognized from football fields away. People told me I was attractive, but I didn't believe it. My daily outfit normally consisted of brown hiking boots, loose jeans, and an oversize brown loose-knit sweater. I began to hide from the world and trudged forward, oblivious to others, in self-critical, introspective misery.

Beyond Ajax, a few close friends kept me hopeful through the long hours of drudgery and self-consciousness that marked high school for me. I did well academically, but only really enjoyed the fiction books and literature I read in my spare time, and wandering the lonely acres of fruit orchards near our house with my mutt,

Milo. I faded away into the books and the orchards whenever possible, and came back only for the few people who proved to be trustworthy and kind, including a couple of friends who lived nearby. I drifted away a bit from my mom and Mark; to a certain extent it was because I didn't want to burden them with my unhappiness. Of course, I loved them both and we often had fun together, but they understood each other readily. With me, I felt it took extra effort. I experienced more resonance with Guy, and confided in him more often.

Amid all of this, my mother and I started clashing. She worked hard every day and came home exhausted; I plodded through school and soccer propelled by a sense of duty and the force of habit. She, to her immeasurable credit, did everything she could to support both me and Mark in our extracurricular activities. But I hated mine and didn't see how I could get out of it. I wanted to learn other things but didn't know how—and didn't feel enough support to improve circumstances. I felt alone; she felt tired. We did not understand each other. Each of us thought the other was being difficult. Guy, during particularly unpleasant exchanges, would sit back and wryly remark, in his mischievous way, that we were too similar. He was Irish and tended, even in the midst of conflict, to provide observations, advice, or ribald commentary like a PEZ dispenser, depending on his mood. Both of us would look at him, unimpressed by his contribution, as he leaned back and took a sip of his beer. He would simply look back and raise his eyebrows.

"What? It's true."

Sip.

❧

Around Christmastime in 1998, when I was sixteen, my mom gave me a present, thinking it would help me. She had given me little surprises before, including the magazines *Seventeen* and *Cosmopolitan*, supposing I would enjoy them. She was right—I did. I read the articles and evaluated the models like an investigator, trying to figure out what "pretty" was and how the hell I could get there.

But that Christmas, the gift was different.

It was a book with a multicolored cover. My mom often shared books with both me and Mark. She had been really into yoga and New Age topics recently; I expected a book on meditation or Eastern thought. But I opened it and saw all of the pages were blank. My brow furrowed and my eyebrows rose. "It's a journal? Thanks, Mom . . ."

"It's a *gratitude* journal," my mom clarified. "This is so you can write down the things you're grateful for. It's easy to get sad or down when you don't realize how many good things are happening. A gratitude journal makes you more aware. What I'd like you to do is write down five things every day that you are grateful for. It doesn't have to be something special or complicated. You could just say, 'I'm grateful for clouds' or 'for grass' . . . just as long as you get five things down."

I looked at her. This sounded an awful lot like homework.

But I recognized gentle kindness when I saw it, even if I acted prickly and unmoved, so I decided to try it. The first evening I wrote in the book, I said thank-you to God for five things that day, including petting a light tan horse. I began to keep the journal faithfully, writing in it every evening. Sometimes I wrote more than five things.

Within a week or so of starting the journal, one thing popped up almost every day in my entries: excitement about an upcoming trip with Michael to Mardi Gras in New Orleans. In a few weeks, during mid-February, Mark and I would fly into San Antonio, see Michael's new house for the first time, and then drive with him to New Orleans. We would be there for the culmination of the huge Mardi Gras celebrations on the day before Catholic Lent began, the revelry of Fat Tuesday. I could not wait, and the journal percolated with my delight.

NEW ORLEANS

Unfortunately, at the end of January my grandma Yates, Michael's mother, Mary, suddenly became gravely ill. Just a couple weeks before the trip to Mardi Gras, she died. Michael was in Louisiana; he had been spending time with her. Mark and I talked with him on the phone a day later and he sounded devastated.

I wanted to miss Grandma, to honor her passing with sorrow; but I couldn't. I felt nothing! I shivered only in a chilly unease, the most distant cousin to sadness. She was family. Her life and blood helped make me, for crying out loud. But I simply didn't know her that well—and couldn't cry. There was no doubt, however, that the long-awaited trip to Mardi Gras now looked dark indeed.

Even our mom, who normally didn't seem to feel much for Michael beyond anger and disgust, expressed genuine sympathy for him. She knew that he and his mom had been unusually close and supportive of each other. She seemed almost grateful for the opportunity to deliver us, like a present, to him at this time of his life, and encouraged both Mark and me: "You guys will go see your dad and have a great time. It will do him some good, too, to have you two with him now. You'll be able to help him feel better." I didn't want to see Michael cry. That would be so sad! I didn't like it when anyone cried. And how could we enjoy Mardi Gras—how could he enjoy Mardi Gras—knowing that Grandma Yates was gone?

Two weeks later, Mark and I arrived in San Antonio, Texas. Michael picked us up, full of hugs and broad grins. His eyes had a tinge of sadness and his smiles fluttered, but he seemed happy—if only for the moment. The very next day, Valentine's Day, we drove the eight hours to New Orleans and stopped by to see Grandpa Yates. Grandpa said hi to us, but he was not, either this time or any other, very talkative. He mainly just spoke to Michael. Neither Mark nor I knew what to say, so we just went outside. We tried to keep out from underfoot, away from the heavy darkness that pervaded the house, and played in the backyard. I dreaded the next step—going with Michael to see Grandma's grave.

As we got ready to leave, Michael asked Grandpa whether he wanted to go, even coaxing him a bit, but Grandpa did not. Instead, he cried and insisted that Mike, as he called my dad, leave immediately, in case the weather took a turn for the worse and it rained.

I have rarely felt so uncomfortable, so porous and sensitive to other people's feelings, and yet unable to help in any way, as on that drive. Michael's jaw was uncharacteristically tense; he was mostly silent. It seemed like being in that old house with his father had opened the floodgates of memory.

Mark and I were both extremely sensitive. We retreated into our respective caves when anyone was upset, especially adults. Our mom's personal relationships were unstable. They taught us that change lurked just outside of her contentment. If she was angry or sad, she might leave the man she was with. The three of us, quite literally, might move to a completely different place if she was unhappy. That kind of emotional volatility had made me intensely anxious. This time was different because it was Michael, but the effect was similar. In fact, it was slightly worse: I didn't know what he might do.

I trembled and glanced at my brother to make sure he was doing all right. He was diligently staring out the window. We stayed quiet to prevent further ripples in the already disturbed water. If someone spoke, it was softly. By the time we got to the cemetery, my father was just barely holding it together. He was Dad suddenly; I felt bad for thinking of him as Michael, for distancing myself when it seemed like so much that was deeply important to him had been taken away.

He had insisted on getting flowers for Grandma and knelt there at the foot of her grave, just crying. Mark and I looked at each other, distraught and confused. We were pretty good at adapting, balancing, and making people feel better. But we didn't know what to do to fix *this*. And he was so sad! The sky was grey; the cemetery was quiet; everything had the aura of a place forgotten—by relatives, the city, the world entirely. And there was Dad, all alone and remembering. Mark and I couldn't see how to ease his pain. So we stood an awkward distance away, holding back tears for him, unwilling to infringe on his privacy but unable to leave.

Eventually Dad stood up heavily and, sniffing a little, wiped his face. He looked at us and seemed to realize that we, Mark and I, were distressed and trying to be good. He moved toward us.

"Thank you for waiting for me. I wanted to talk to Grandma. And, Mark, Tiffany, I want you to know that I love you very, very much."

His tone of voice was heavy, full of years. He often said (or wrote) similar things, but this time it seemed like he wanted it to really sink in. I didn't know how to respond; my heart was bursting. I just remember staring at the cemetery trees and thinking, *Why did God make life like this?*

Mark was the hero who managed a reply: "I love you too, Dad! I'm really sorry Grandma died."

"Me too, Mark," he replied.

He gave us each a hug as we walked to the car. I started to relax; the hugs were like sunshine after a storm. We got in the car and drove a few blocks in silence; then Michael forced a smile and, trying to be cheerful, said, "What do y'all think? Do you want to go to Bacchus tonight?"

The enormous evening procession of the Krewe of Bacchus was one of the highlights of the Mardi Gras season. Krewes were groups of people who spent the whole year preparing for the festivities of the narrow window before the Lenten season. As I understood it, they often even did charity work throughout the community. The larger and older the krewe, the more likely they had really cool "throws" (necklaces, doubloons, etc.), outstanding floats in their parades, and a long history of celebrity royalty. We had both been to Mardi Gras in New Orleans with Michael before—another brief trip—and Bacchus was one of our favorite parades.

Michael mustered enthusiasm and moved full-steam ahead into the conversation, detailing the upcoming events. For Bacchus that year, he informed us, Jim Belushi was going to be king. I had no idea who Jim Belushi was, or why he was famous, but it was the parade of Bacchus! Whoever was king, as far as I was concerned, it was bound to be a good time.

The parade brought all of us back into the Mardi Gras spirit; the enthusiasm of the crowd was contagious. Everything seemed almost normal. The next day we went to Orpheus, another exceptionally large super-krewe with a huge parade. Sandra Bullock was in that procession; Mark loved her, and all three of us were on high alert for her float on his behalf. As it turned out, we didn't need to look that hard. Her arrival was preceded by shouting and cheers that went up before her ornate float like a bow wave, and then there she was, throwing necklaces and doubloons from on high. Everyone was trying to catch something that Sandra threw. Mark acted like young man on a mission; Michael and I had a hard time keeping track of him as he raced through the hordes of people. He chased her float for what seemed like miles. Finally, when I started to feel genuinely exhausted by all of the running and jostling and shouting, Mark strode back through the crowd, like royalty, to me and Michael. He had caught beads from both Sandra and a Playboy Playmate. Michael laughed, looking at Mark's huge smile, and shouted gleefully, trying to be heard through the din surrounding us, "Good for you, Mark!"

Every necklace had a lineage, a story; hanging and sparkling around my brother's neck was a history book of the night. He would pry one apart from the mass and tell us exactly how and where he got it. As Mark briefed us on the escapades of each block, Michael beamed and his eyes sparkled. He loved New Orleans and the fact that he had now taken us to Mardi Gras a couple times. It was a miniature tradition, and he loved tradition. He kept repeating how we "could remember this forever." Maybe our mom was right and this fast-paced trip so soon after Grandma's passing was really good for my dad. He had not mentioned her much since going to her grave site the day before, and certainly didn't seem to be overcome with grief. Mardi Gras, and our presence, appeared to be an effective distraction.

～ᘯ～

That night, after Orpheus, we headed to Slidell, Louisiana, just outside of New Orleans, to see my Grandpa's country property—which is to say, his parcel in the swamp. It served as his getaway, and Michael often gave us updates on the phone about what Grandpa had done to the place. Grandpa had built the house himself, but aside from the independence and ingenuity it represented, the structure on the property was one of the ugliest things I had ever seen. The rectangular two-story form, built from grey cinderblocks, alternated, depending on one's angle and the time of day, between looking like a prison, an abandoned crack house, and a stranded seagoing vessel of some sort. Aesthetics was obviously not high on my Grandpa's list, or else beyond his capacity as a builder. The good thing was, you could do anything on Grandpa's Slidell property and no one would care. We could throw rocks, drive tractors, and fish in the pond. There was only one rule: Be careful of the alligators. For those reasons, Mark and I loved the property, and Michael never said a negative thing about it. He was full of praise and encouragement for Grandpa Yates's construction experiment.

While Michael drove us to Grandpa's place after Orpheus—it must have been close to or just after midnight—I stared into the black night, thinking about the parade we'd left and Grandpa's house ahead. There was a lot of traffic (most of it Mardi Gras–related), and the narrow lanes over Lake Pontchartrain contributed to tension between tired drivers. When the lanes somehow opened up—I don't remember how, we might have passed an accident—a small sedan with two people cut my dad off—badly. Michael honked and glared at them in a sudden, myopic anger. The driver, a young man, flipped him off. The other young man in the passenger seat followed suit.

Michael looked as if he could kill those two men. As they sped up in the opening traffic, Michael turned on his high beams and pursued them with astonishing ferocity. We approached a hundred miles an hour, right on the rear bumper of those guys. If the driver had hit his brakes we would have all been toast. Mark and I got scared. The young guys in front of us got scared. Michael, on the other hand, was on a mission. To do what, I don't know. But whatever it entailed, it didn't matter that we were in the car with him or that the scenery was screaming by. I genuinely thought he was going to ram their car into something and beat the living daylights out of them. He tailed them with his bright lights until they flew off an exit. Obviously, it was not to go to their destination—just to get away from him: The exit was, due to construction, a dead end. Michael had none of their escape; he took the turn on two wheels.

The boys, seeing our vehicle following them off the freeway, were presumably panicked now. Their car's movement certainly suggested it. Forced into a U-turn in the dust of the end of the road, their car stopped momentarily. Our car raced toward them and skidded to a stop, stirring up dust that floated into view above the dashboard in the dark night. My heart was pounding; I was scared stiff. I didn't think this chase could get crazier—but it did. Michael gripped his door handle to exit. Was he going to fight? I grabbed my door handle to follow. Whatever was going to happen, I wanted to help. He was out of control, but he was Dad.

Michael looked over and ordered me, "Stay in the car!" He opened his door with fierce anger; the guys saw him get out. The passenger thumped the driver like, *Leave already!* Michael headed straight for the fray, calling for a fight with every step. It didn't appear to occur to him that they might have a gun or baseball bat or anything else. My body burned. *I'm not staying in here! I'm going to defend him!* I opened my door, which, due to the angle of our rental car, was farther away from their vehicle. As soon as they saw my car door open, the driver, with renewed alarm, accelerated again. Apparently it didn't occur to them that the people chasing them were a divorced dad with his teenage children. Why would it? They most likely saw dark figures moving behind high-beam headlights, my father's livid posture silhouetted and anonymous against those bright lights.

I watched their car surge away, gaining speed into the night. They hadn't planned it well; the freeway up ahead was stopped again. If Michael was still going to act crazy and pursue them, they could still be in trouble. There was nowhere to go. I looked at Michael to gauge his level of anger. Was he going to follow?

He turned and saw me standing outside of the car; Mark had, at some point, also gotten out. Michael's movements were slower now, more rational. Whether it was the rising dust, the night air, or the realization that he'd driven miles at top speed in a fit of road rage to intimidate two rude men—whatever anger had taken my dad over had left. He was empty.

We stood looking at each other in the dust, amid the empty construction of the exit, looking at a different and far less festive parade—the slow lights of the freeway. Michael reached for his car door. As he got in, he said, "I told you to stay inside."

"I know . . . but I wanted to help," I responded lamely.

"Me too!" Mark exclaimed, with wide eyes and a cautious expression. Neither of us knew what to make of our father at this moment.

"I'm sorry for what just happened," Michael said, speaking slowly. "I lost control and it was wrong. You should never follow someone like that, and especially never get out of the car if someone follows you." His voice was tired and practiced, like that of a weary scholar. "And I told you to stay in the car."

A few moments later, we pulled out of the dust and dirt. I tried to ease the tension in the car. Michael was quiet, as if he were ashamed—or else disappointed that the guys got away.

"Well," I said, trying to lighten the mood in the car, "I bet those boys don't flip anybody else off again."

Michael's crooked smile flashed, but it didn't touch his eyes.

Mark and I, accustomed to our mom, had never seen anything like Michael's behavior that night—from anyone. His anger was ice-cold and terrifying.

We continued on our trip into the Cajun darkness. The drive was quiet and uneventful for the remainder of the evening; we were all lost in thought and exhausted. I kept glancing at my dad, hoping that he wouldn't notice. Something in me shouted warnings: *This is what happens when you're not honest with yourself!* Maybe he hadn't let Grandma's death sink in. Whatever caused his reaction, he couldn't control it. He was too absorbed and unaware. Something else had ruled him—and I loathed and feared him for it. I wanted to talk about it, to understand. But this didn't seem like the time to discuss it—if ever. He might get mad again. As tired as I was, I perched uncomfortably in my seat for the rest of the drive.

When we arrived in Slidell, we all went straight to bed.

🦇

We spent time with Grandpa the following morning and on the last day of our visit we returned to New Orleans. Michael took us to Café du Monde, a small restaurant in the French Quarter just off of Jackson Square, which is known for its beignets (small, sugary doughnuts), hot chocolate, and coffee. The café is normally crowded at all hours, open as it is twenty-four hours a day year-round, but it feels relaxed and removed from the rest of the city.

Jackson Square itself is a small park in the heart of the old French Quarter—an old and cobblestoned place that is prone to grime and filth, full of fortune-tellers and carriage drivers jostling for the attention of passing tourists. I loved Jackson Square. It felt mysterious, quietly magical. And on one side of it, towering above the fenced lawn and the pandering entertainers like a reclusive king, stands the St. Louis Cathedral. Michael talked about the cathedral as we ate, and we went in—par for the course when it came to churches—to see the sanctuary.

We drove back to San Antonio and, the following day, flew back to California. That was it. In a whirlwind itinerary—as was any trip or visit we ever had with him—in four days we'd packed two Southern states, twenty hours of driving, a world-famous carnival, and visits with family members. Michael always concentrated as many activities and trips as time would allow, and we were carried along in a mad dash of life. For me and Mark, upon returning home, it was just back to school and the normal routine.

I didn't wonder then, but I do now, what Michael felt and thought afterward about that evening in the car: when everything settled into silence—when he had time to think.

INCARNATE WORD

Because my mom traveled locally for work and her schedule didn't often coincide with mine, Guy was the adult who, for the most part, taught me how to drive when I returned to Modesto. I cherished the driving lessons. We escaped! We disappeared for hours into the foothills of the Sierra Nevada Mountains, coursing through the tiny and virtually abandoned mining towns—Coulterville, Jackson, Columbia—collecting the necessary hours I needed behind the wheel. Often we would stop in one of the towns, grab lunch, and walk through the boutique stores. Guy and I talked about everything, in short bursts of honesty. We both vented occasionally throughout the day; our temperaments suited each other. On those day trips, the boiling water in my teenage teakettle cooled to a mild, less self-destructive, and healthier simmer.

On one of those trips with Guy, I caught sight of the Yates family crest for the first time, in a revolving display at a souvenir shop. I pointed it out. It appeared as though there was some truth to the story I'd heard in my childhood. The crest had three gates on it: Two stood in the light of day—and one in the dark of night.

So there it was: the sign of the guards.

The evening and weekend drives with Guy continued; sometimes my mom even had time and let me drive the car with her when we went to the grocery store. (Those short trips with her often made it into the gratitude journal.) On one trip, she teased me all the way home: Apparently the grocery cashier had been hitting on me and I didn't realize it. Mom laughed. "Tiffany, you are *oblivious*! You have no idea when boys are hitting on you—and it happens all the time!"

That wasn't entirely accurate. It very definitely did not happen all the time, and when it did, often I had every idea and chose to play the interaction off, to pretend I was ignorant of the advances. I felt a little uncomfortable when it came to other people in general, and especially with boys. Maybe it was due to Ajax or the low-grade teasing at home; maybe the fact I'd been weirdly twisted somehow while growing up in a broken family. Whatever it was, I was afraid I was intrinsically odd or flawed, and that no one would really like me if they got to know me.

A handsome boy named Malachi, who was as mysterious as his name might suggest, had asked me out recently at school and I said yes. He had dark features and practiced martial arts; he was, in fact, the first one to ask me whom I was actually interested in. For whatever reason, that relationship lasted only a couple weeks; however, it was enough that I started paying attention to boys, especially those who moved confidently and had a steady gaze. Malachi was a muscular young man with a spiritual streak, sensitive, even a little troubled—and I discovered I liked that.

I turned seventeen and got my driver's license, but I was still somewhat socially withdrawn. I felt beaten down by depression, confusion, and lack of purpose. When all of that latent frustration and uncertainty combined with the ever-simmering conflict at home with my mom, nothing seemed good. My experiences with Ajax had prompted me to not trust people as much—or at all—for support. Finally, though, there was a minor reprieve: I managed to get out of that soccer league. (Hallelujah!)

Despite that small victory, I didn't feel comfortable at school; I couldn't relax at home. Existence was a pressure cooker, getting hotter and hotter, with no relief in sight. The gratitude journal helped me to be more aware of little things that my mom and friends did to try to help me, but it couldn't dispel the aching, desperate aggravation. The tension eased only rarely: when I was in the foothills with Guy, or when I visited Michael.

Our trip to Mardi Gras was the first time in a long time that I'd felt excited about what I was doing: from going to the parades in New Orleans in the evenings to just knowing that Mark and I were helping Michael feel better after Grandma's death. Moreover, we'd seen Michael's new house—the first he had ever purchased—and both of us liked it. It was fascinating seeing something that he considered nice enough to make his own, like viewing his deepest values in a tidy little package. While we were there we all—Mark, Michael, and I—started calling the house itself "Allensworth," as if it were a country estate (i.e., "Let's stop by Allensworth beforehand . . ."). What started out as convenient shorthand inadvertently created a sense of home.

I loved the style and tone of life in Texas. San Antonio is one of the largest cities in the state. It spreads out like a hot, asphalt glacier over the landscape, but manages to feel like a small town. It has a pervasive feeling of space, as though one could conceivably pull off the freeway, make a couple turns, and be at a vast ranch. Cities have personalities, as anyone who has been to more than one can attest. If New York constantly chatters with the discordant prattle of a crazed lunatic, sometimes vicious and occasionally profound, San Antonio sits on the other side of the spectrum. It sits back in the rocking chair of its hills, breathes, wonders, and has a pleasant underlying sense of just *being*. Less of a rush. Less of a frantic effort to prove. There is, within San Antonio, an indescribable something that is radiant and very quiet.

That trip to see my dad, and the happiness I experienced while gallivanting around Texas and Louisiana, threw my despair while in California into high relief. Life with Michael was movement; life here was stagnant and stale.

One day, in a fit of annoyance at my behavior, my mom locked me out of the house. I didn't understand—I didn't feel like I'd done anything wrong. To this day, I can't recall why she did it. All I remember is her smirking face looking at me from the kitchen window. An acute sense of injustice assailed me. I felt intensely misunderstood. At that moment I had had enough. My will rose up and for once it was crystal clear and brutally strong:

I wanted *out*.

Out of the house. Out of Modesto. Out of this life.

I thought about what I could do. Run away. Move in with friends. Even—although I wouldn't admit it to anyone—kill myself. Confused and unhappy, I considered anything just to change something. There was nothing to keep me there—certainly not a busy senior year at Beyer.

I remembered my dad telling me and my brother, "Tiff, Mark, you are always welcome at my house. If you ever want to live here, just let me know. Mom and I will make that happen."

I decided.

$$\sim$$

I approached my mom later that evening, almost quivering inside at the hailstorm I was about to release. She was not going to like this.

"Mom," I said.

"Yeah?"

"I've decided that I want to go live with Dad."

Silence.

She looked at me. "Okay . . . Are you sure that's what you want to do? It's your senior year."

"Yes. I'm sure."

"Okay. Call him and let him know." She had her game face on. The stoicism was deliberate and concrete, but made me anxious. I knew she was feeling something, but I couldn't tell what. And I hadn't mentioned this decision to Michael at all. It might not even be possible.

That night, alone in my bedroom in California, I felt the walls of my tiny world crashing down on me. I had destroyed with one pronouncement everything I knew. I felt completely overwhelmed by the task of building a new life.

When Mark and I had visited Michael in San Antonio earlier that year, he'd mentioned that the city of San Antonio was named after Saint Anthony of Padua.

"Saint Anthony," he had said, "is the patron saint of lost things."

He described the concept of a patron saint: someone who during their life became associated with a particular part of life or experience and, after they died, helped other people with things related to that experience. In his life—the legend goes—Saint Anthony had a book stolen, prayed for its return, and the thief was moved to return it.

I liked the idea of Saint Anthony. Lying in my bed, I reflected: *I have no idea who I am. I don't know what I'm supposed to do. Since Saint Anthony is the patron saint of lost things, maybe being in his city can help me.* I prayed: "Dear Saint Anthony, I don't know you very well, but please help me find myself."

My dad seemed excited about finally having one of his kids living with him. It was, perhaps, many a divorced dad's dream come true. In a whirlwind he reviewed schooling options in San Antonio. I had two choices: a definite admission into the public high school in the city center with a rough (but improving) reputation, or the slim chance of being accepted into a small, private all-girls Roman Catholic high school about five minutes from his new house. He strongly favored the Catholic school. It was closer, he liked the fact that it was Catholic, and he felt it would be safer.

I had never gone to a Catholic school, but I was open to the idea. My only hesitation lay in the fact that I really didn't know that much about Catholicism in general. I could get around and look like I knew what I was doing after all the years of going to Mass with my dad and brother, but just hoped that nobody asked too many questions.

In early August my dad called, elated with the news: The small Catholic school accepted me. It had come down to the wire, with him scrambling to make it all happen. The success electrified him.

"Tiffany, do you still have that Bible I gave you?"

"Yes, I do."

"Okay, you probably ought to bring that. You're going to have theology class. And I don't know . . . you might need a Bible on the first day. At any rate, it would be a good thing to have."

"Okay, I'll bring it. Thanks, Dad."

I hung up the phone and sighed. Theology? I'd never had a theology class. I hoped I didn't flunk it. What if I didn't know enough about the Bible?

Over the next several days, my mom and Michael both worked hard to help me get ready to move. Mark stayed in the background, a little unsure why I even wanted to go. He knew that Mom and I had not been getting along, but I never shared my reasons for leaving. I didn't want to burden him with more negativity; we were, after years together, very protective of each other's feelings.

I felt ashamed, as if I were abandoning him in a way. I wasn't trying to be selfish, but I could not take this action and maintain a host of sensitivities. I had to turn it all off, close my eyes to any sadness, and charge ahead. Something told me it was the right thing to do. Guy sensed my need to focus and act; he stayed quiet and supportive in the background, and it was not until years later that he confided to me that my mom cried for three nights straight after I announced I wanted to leave.

With days until school started, I left my family and Beyer High with its sprawling campus in California for the small Catholic school—and my dad—in San Antonio, Texas.

SAN ANTONIO

Two days later, I landed on the tarmac in San Antonio. My dad, all smiles and excitement, greeted me at the terminal and gave me a big hug. I felt excited, but a little awkward too. I wasn't quite sure what to do. This was Dad. But what was "everyday" with him? How should I act? I thought I should be extra polite and say thank-you a lot.

"Hi, Dad! Nice to see you! Thank you so much for helping me move here!"

"Of course, honey!" He gave me another huge hug and talked about practical matters as we headed together toward the exit, walking side by side. Our strides matched perfectly, but that was the only harmony I sensed. Maybe it would start to feel normal soon.

A blast of heat assailed us as we passed through the airport's automatic sliding doors, and San Antonio greeted us in full sun-drenched glory. The parking lot was within view, and I immediately picked out my dad's huge forest-green Yukon amid the smaller cars.

"I thought we could drop by the house so you can see your room," he said, smiling broadly. "Then we can run to the commissary and Post Exchange—PX—on Fort Sam Houston and get any food you might want. There's not much at the house."

He had always loved shopping on military posts, convinced that they offered better prices. Since he'd retired from the U.S. Army, he retained—and relished—the privilege of shopping on post. He continued. "Tomorrow we can go out again and pick up all of the stuff that you'll need for school, including your uniform."

I suddenly realized that this must be as weird for him as it was for me. This was the first time he would have a child in his house who needed to get to school on time. It was clear that he took the responsibility seriously and was nervous about both the move and the school transition going well. (The ever-looming albeit distant wrath of my mom probably didn't help reduce his anxiety.)

We drove away from the airport, entering the highway easily and going a couple miles before he took the exit for Hildebrand Avenue, a gradual incline that peaked at an intersection. The light was red; we stopped and waited. He pointed to a building on a hillside to the right.

"That," he said, "is your new school."

I looked, all of a sudden hyperalert.

Oh, God. This is going to be a complete disaster.

It looked like a fortress—anything but welcoming. Brown buildings topped the hill with a kind of finality. Nothing about it looked nice. My hopes for life at this school, maintained with ease when it was just a dream of the future, disappeared in a puff of reality. Searching inside my heart, I tried to find confidence—and suddenly wondered whether I had made a giant mistake.

Incarnate Word High School, known locally simply as Incarnate Word, is on a high hill in the center of San Antonio, overlooking one of the main highways of the city and some of the most expensive real estate in the region. It is situated between two universities: the University of the Incarnate Word to the east and Trinity University to the southwest. The high school's administration building proudly displays Incarnate Word's complicated school seal but, oddly enough, the school mascot is not displayed anywhere. It is the modest—and, according to the rival coaching staffs of Antonian and Providence, unquestionably lame—shamrock.

The light turned green and we drove on. Michael pointed out the entrance to the San Antonio Zoo and, after we passed a bridge, mentioned an extraordinarily beautiful statue in the adjacent historical cemetery: "It's kind of hidden, so you have to watch very closely . . . ah! There it is, see it?"

The Yukon drifted a little in the lane as Michael leaned to the right to get a better view. A headless female form, the angel figure was sculpted striding forward, the marble rendered so expertly that it no longer looked like stone but thick, rich folds of cloth. Huge wings expanded behind the statue, the plumage of heaven frozen forever in time.

"Wow," I exclaimed, "that's gorgeous! It should be in a prettier place. What's it called?"

"*Winged Victory.*" He pronounced the name clearly, as if savoring the words. "It's a copy of the original, which is in the Louvre."

I murmured the name to myself, hunching forward far into the seat to watch its white form dwindle into the park and the trees. *Winged Victory.*

Then suddenly we took a left turn and were on his street.

The house was located in central San Antonio near Broadway, a main thoroughfare that led from Alamo Heights, a somewhat ritzy section north of Allensworth, to the center of downtown near the famed Alamo itself. I had been to his house during Mardi Gras earlier that year, but this time I looked at it and the neighborhood with the fresh perspective of a new resident. Mature trees sheltered small, well-maintained homes. Broad streets met one another with the gentle, slow feeling of communion. The tension of speed was nowhere to be found.

The facade of the house was a neutral white, and unassuming. Four unpretentious columns in front guarded a simple and comfortable porch. It was a forgettable house—unless one paid close attention and noticed the care with which things were designed and proportioned, and the pleasant spaces nestled beneath and around its wooden framework. So many houses are designed with only aesthetics in mind, as developers give homes a cursory dose of curb appeal: Porches three feet deep are useless. Little insults to the human body—and the proper space it requires to relax—accumulate in many modern homes and make them unfit for true comfort. Interiors become hollow caverns with unused spaces, or tight trails through piles of possessions; exteriors are similarly warped: pretentiously grand or flat like a pug-nosed dog that can't breathe properly. Michael's house, however, was a happy little creation: modest and clean.

When I exited the Yukon, my shoes landed on part gravel, part grass. Standing still in the front yard, I gazed up at the large, shady tree, its trunk bizarrely forked, and smiled. *I'm here!* I grabbed my backpack from the front seat and shut the door.

"Tiffany!" my dad scolded. He leaned around the Yukon and his eyebrows came together in a dark frown. "Don't slam the door!"

I stopped suddenly, alarmed by the irritation on his face. A ball of fear rose up within me. I had no idea I'd slammed the door. I looked at the Yukon, evaluating it for any damage, and then back at him. He leaned into the cavernous rear storage area to pull out my larger bag, but his posture and quick moves suggested he was still annoyed. I took a step back away from the car and waited, stiff-legged and awkward.

"I'm sorry, Dad. I didn't realize I slammed it." I said, as I walked over slowly to help carry the bags in.

"Well"—he hauled a bag out and shouldered his own back-pack—"just think about things like that. Try to take care of stuff. I don't want to damage the truck."

"Okay. I'll be careful. I'm . . . sorry." I glanced down at the grass and then back at the Yukon, which sat there like an imperturbable green elephant.

As he fumbled for the right key, I tried to calm down. *Relax. Everything will be okay.* His annoyance was just a small blip in what would be a good move, a great decision. *It isn't the end of the world. Steady.* My heart, though, still fluttered. The warm afternoon, oddly enough, helped slow my spiraling concern. Even anxiety cannot race pell-mell through thick southern heat. There was sudden movement and clatter at the door—the lock turned—and Michael stepped into the house.

We went inside, the front door creaking with a gentle groan as we entered. I found my smile again. It sounded like coming home.

Because the house was so small, the homecoming tour was short. We walked a few steps into the back bedroom, which was to be mine, and I immediately loved it. I'd seen the room briefly when Mark and I came blazing through San Antonio for Mardi Gras, but all of us had fallen asleep in the living room that evening, amid a pile of blankets and pillows, watching a movie as if it were a sleepover party. Michael had cleaned the entire house up a lot since then. At the time it had been messy; he had not quite settled in. But now there were no boxes blocking the windows, no piles of uniforms and button-down shirts on the furniture, still on hangers but not hanging. Spacious and peaceful, the back bedroom had gleaming hardwood floors and four large windows. There was a wooden bed in the middle, a small nightstand, and a chest of drawers. Aside from those items, it was completely bare. None of the furniture matched, but, as it was all plain and strictly functional, the overall effect was coherent and pleasant.

Michael said, "This is the nicest, biggest room, and I want you to have it. I'll sleep in the front bedroom."

"But there's no bed in there!" I protested.

"That's okay. My back feels better when I sleep on the floor. You can use this chest of drawers," he said, "and we can get another one if you need it."

"Oh, no, Dad! That one will be fine. Thank you."

He turned around in the room and moved toward the far wall. "There's an interesting story related to this house, and this room in particular," he said. "I bought this house from an elderly woman. Her husband had built it after World War II. She was a very nice old lady but couldn't live by herself anymore. She had to sell the house, but wanted me to understand how important it was to her."

I wondered whether this story had played a part in why he bought the house. It seemed to inspire him.

"Many years ago," he continued, "her son got seriously ill. The doctors didn't think he would live. The little old lady, who was Catholic, prayed to the Blessed Virgin Mary for intercession, and promised that if Mary would help her son live, she would always have a space in her home for her. Her son miraculously recovered and surprised everybody. Even the doctors! That same week, the woman had a small alcove made in the master bedroom.

"This"—he gestured—"is it."

It was a small recess in the eastern wall, no more than two feet tall, and sculpted like an archway. The woman had designed it specifically to hold a statue of Mary, like one might find in a chapel or church. There was a statue in it even now.

"I keep a small statue of Mary here," he continued, "because I think it's the right thing to do. She was such a nice lady, and I want to help her keep her promise."

His loyalty to her struck me as very sweet, especially given that she would most likely never know about it. The tiny alcove gave the room some character. The space looked like a room in a convent, or maybe a military dorm, but that was part of why I loved it: Clutter, the nonsense and commercial refuse of living, was absent. I'd always preferred simplicity. Every item ought to serve a practical or beautiful purpose, and contribute to a feeling of wholesome well-being.

After a few hours in the new house, I began to feel excited about life again. I unpacked and established my space in minor ways—a jacket in the closet, toothbrush in the small bathroom—as if I were a gardener immersing a plant clipping to grow new roots.

That night, we ate dinner at Earl Abel's, a fantastic country-style restaurant right around the corner. The walls of the expansive single dining room were covered in humorous signs announcing things like, "Our clock will never be stolen. The employees are always watching it." Michael and I talked about the school and procuring necessities. My nervousness disappeared during the hot meal and proactive planning with him; by the time dessert came around, I felt downright confident. With my belly full, I basked in the contentment that follows traveling long distances—the calm, cheerful sensation of finally being still.

The next day, we ran errands to get everything I needed for school. While purchasing pieces of my uniform—which consisted of very specific styles of green plaid skirts, white shirts, knee-high socks, gray sweaters, and a lengthy bit of plaid fabric that was somehow worn as a tie—we realized I needed shoes as well. Only two shoe styles constituted approved footwear at Incarnate Word: plain black penny loafers and black-and-white saddle oxfords, which reminded me of a Holstein cow. Michael purchased one set of each so I could have some variety. I had never worn either kind of shoe before in my life; both of them looked very prim and proper.

That evening, I put out my new school uniform and lined up my shoes. I wrestled with the loafers to put a single penny in their respective black leather notches. Michael watched, smiling, while I sat cross-legged on the floor and tried to jam the penny in the first one. Encountering some difficulty, I looked up at him and we both laughed. Exasperated, I exclaimed, "This isn't a good sign, Dad!"

It occurred to me that it might be kind of cool to be able to wear shoes that we'd both "worked" on, almost like good luck, so I asked, "Do you want to put the penny in the other one?"

"Sure, honey!" he replied. He grinned and crouched next to me, grabbing the other shoe.

PINS AND BADGES

Michael seemed to think problems might plague my shift from a large public school to a private Catholic one. I suspected that he worried I wouldn't fit in. But I'd changed schools a lot growing up while Randall served as minister to different Methodist churches; in twelve years I had gone to seven schools—though Michael had never been around for that. Being the new kid was almost normal to me.

The morning of my first day, I took inventory of my school supplies methodically and checked them off the list the school administration provided. I enjoyed picking out which notebooks and pens to bring. Michael, on the other hand, was unusually nervous and active. He fussed with his tie and paced the house repeatedly, double-checking things as we got ready.

I put on the green plaid uniform for the first time and actually liked not having to pick out an outfit to wear. The peculiar tie was impossible, though. I fumbled with it for a while and then just gave up. *The uniform store should provide instructions for these clothes!* Shoving the tie in my backpack, I decided to ask somebody before class how to put it on. Meanwhile, Michael busied himself with getting lunch together and watching the clock very closely. We finally got out the door and clambered, with a heaving of backpacks, his and mine, into the Yukon.

The first moment was quiet. The engine turned over and there was a subtle lurch as the Yukon, with a floating sensation, eased over the dip in the driveway and into the main street. Even though we were father and daughter, original and namesake, because of all the years and all the miles, we weren't much more than strangers. A little bit of that awkwardness crept into the air now.

He finally spoke: "Now, Tiffany, I want to say that since this is the first day, it's a good thing to just be quiet. Just be quiet and watch, okay? Learn. Watch what the other girls do until you get the hang of how things work. Understand?" He looked at me meaningfully.

I looked back at him. "Oh, yeah, I understand."

But I felt surprised. He didn't give advice often. Or maybe he did and I just didn't listen. I turned ahead and looked through the broad windshield at the cars lined up in front of us in the left-turn lane. *Why is he saying this so strongly?* As we pulled up the steep drive to the administration building of my new high school, my confidence wavered, like when I'd first glimpsed the sprawling property and its imposing structures from the exit ramp at the bottom of the hill. What on earth was Michael afraid I'd say? Did he think I was normally obnoxious and outspoken? Did I not come across well?

I looked out the window and, with a plummeting sensation, saw that all of the other girls were wearing their green plaid ties in neat little knots. Not only that, but all of the ties were covered in shiny pins and badges.

I grimaced. Resolving to make it through this day, I reached for my backpack.

My dad looked at me and inhaled deeply. His nervousness had not dissipated. He sat a little askew, trying to face me as much as the captain's seat would allow. I realized he was afraid I was going to have a bad day at school. *Oh, my God. What if I have a bad day at school!* My heart seized for a moment. He leaned forward, gave me a big hug as if he had done it every day of my life, and said, "Okay, Tiff, I love you! I'll be here this afternoon to pick you up."

"Okay, Dad. I love you too. Have a good day at work."

I got out, turned from the Yukon, and faced the school. Walking up through the large courtyard and plot of grass to the main building, I noticed one thing immediately, and to this day the feeling of walking up that hill is fresh in my mind: It was steep! I turned around once to wave back at Michael and then, unzipping my backpack, grabbed that pesky tie. The exertion of hiking forced me to think about something else besides my newfound nervousness, and for that I felt very grateful. Breathing heavily by the time I got to the side door, I entered the administration building.

There was no one inside.

Whoa. Where are all the people?

Tentatively, I walked forward, surprised by the unexpected quiet. My shoes sounded really loud in the silence. There were girls outside, I thought. Why were the halls empty? I was expecting jostling crowds, aggressive tones, and obnoxious attitudes, like in the California schools. I was prepared for low-level threat anxiety, as if vulnerabilities were everywhere. Not violence exactly, but judgment—an ignorant jock, a mean classmate, a snarky girl. One always had to be on guard in the California hallways.

Keep your head up.

It came back to me suddenly, crashing through the years: On the first day at Beyer, I was a high-strung freshman with a brand-new backpack walking the halls of a small city. Utterly terrified, I tried to find my first class (without looking up or making eye contact with anyone, of course), and my heartbeat rang loud in my own ears. Suddenly a voice had whispered in my ear. I glanced up just in time to see an older boy, my next-door neighbor Nick, passing by. He was a senior, very handsome and popular, and I hadn't even seen him.

"Keep your head up," he repeated. He flashed a smile—encouraging—and continued walking, disappearing into the fast, confusing vortex of rushing students.

I consciously raised my chin, gave a quick silent thanks to Nick, and set out to find my first class. My steps in the shiny new penny loafers sounded against the hard floor and rang down the halls. I thought of my dad's advice as I walked: *Just be quiet.*

Finally I began to see a few people, and I searched for someone, anyone who seemed nice enough to approach about the tie dilemma. After going up a flight of stairs, I caught sight of a tall blond girl with curly hair and a big grin who just happened to be standing by the classroom I had to enter. She looked friendly, and her tie was practically covered in tiny multicolored pins. I took a breath and walked up to her.

"Um, excuse me; I'm new here. I feel kind of stupid about this, but I don't know how to put this tie on the right way," I said, showing her the fistful of fabric. *Oh, please don't be mean.* I inwardly winced.

"Oh, my gosh! These ties are the most ridiculous things! It took me three days to get it right. It's pretty easy once you get the hang of it, though," the blond girl said, taking her tie off and demonstrating right there in the hall. "It's just right-over-left and then left-over-right. It's called a square knot. Here, try."

I tried and fumbled a bit.

"Close, but it's prettier this way." The girl corrected it diplomatically. "And when you get your initials on your tie, if you do the knot properly, the initials will show." I looked at the girl's tie. Sure enough, clean white initials and the girl's class year were resting on the tiny plaid corner. I wondered how I got those. I had exhausted my first burst of courage, though, and decided not to ask.

"Thank you so much!" I said sincerely. "I really appreciate it."

"No problem! I'm Meagan, by the way. What's your name?"

"Tiffany."

"Are you in Mr. Foss's class?"

"Yes, I am!"

"So am I. Here, let's go. You can sit by me, and I'll introduce you to some of the other girls." She opened the door and together we entered the classroom. Meagan ended up being the perfect person to approach—she knew everyone and was very boisterous and bubbly. I knew my classmates' names before the teacher entered the room, and as class started, Meagan leaned over to say, "If you have trouble with the tie tomorrow, just let me know."

I smiled and nodded. This might work out after all. . . .

꙳

When Michael picked me up after school, my tie was on properly and I was smiling. He lost years when he saw me, clearly relieved.

"So how was your first day?" he said with a smile.

"It was great!" I launched into a debriefing that lasted through the drive home and into dinner. When I mentioned the initials on the girls' ties, he raised his eyebrows and looked at my tie.

"Hmm. Maybe we can find out about them," he said.

The tally of highlights included being enrolled in the Latin course. I'd requested it before school started, but it wasn't clear at the time whether there would be enough students to fill the class. I wanted to be able to understand engravings on ancient ruins, to decipher the little secret meanings behind normal words. That morning, when I found out Latin had enough students for the class to commence, a thrill surged through me; however, that same excitement hit a brick wall in the early afternoon when I realized who the instructor was—a nun.

Priests and nuns intimidated me—anyone who devoted his or her entire life and being to God. After hearing stories about nuns as teachers, I wasn't sure what to expect. I had visions of black fabric and holy fury. Some of the sisters at Incarnate Word had said hello to me in the hallways—and they were very polite—but the interactions were brief. When I voiced my fears to my dad, he reassured me.

"Just focus, work hard, and be nice. Some of the best instructors I ever had were nuns."

But the damage was done, now inked on my course schedule casually: *Sr. Mary.*

❦

Sister Mary, the great unknown, was a tall, matronly woman with a calm presence. She spoke in a precise and steady manner that suggested an intensely introspective nature. I was careful the first few weeks, speaking only when spoken to in class and studying dutifully outside of it, but she proved to be a very kind instructor. She appreciated discipline and attention to detail, and I had no problem with that. Latin quickly became one of my favorite classes.

As an instructor, Sister Mary did not publicize the fact that she was a nun. She didn't wear a traditional habit or talk about being a sister. But when she spoke about Jesus, a palpable adoration emanated from her. I could almost feel it vibrate in the room. Her devotion manifested itself as patience with the class and a profound appreciation for learning. When she described Jesus, Sister Mary closed her eyes and disappeared into herself: "The name of our school comes from a verse in the Bible in the Book of John: 'The Word was made flesh and dwelt among us.' Jesus himself," she continued, "*is* the Incarnate Word. The motto of our school is Latin: *Amor Meus. Amor Meus* means 'My Love,' and refers to the love that we feel for Jesus, our savior."

She opened her eyes, only to look at something very far away. God was taking Sister Mary somewhere again. She disappeared out of the classroom on occasion, her body always present, but her spirit now and then soaring on faith, contracting only enough to bring her back on occasion to answer a student's question about Latin, the school, or tiny three-leafed clovers.

"The shamrock mascot is symbolic of God. The three leaves represent the Holy Trinity."

This was already old news to me. Throughout Incarnate Word, students learned very quickly that "lucky" four-leafed clovers were not shamrocks. A shamrock had three leaves and that was it. The legend went that Saint Patrick used the shamrock, already considered sacred by the pagan druids in Ireland, to teach people about the concept of God as the Trinity: the Father, Son, and Holy Ghost.

❦

Soon after I moved to San Antonio, Guy and my mom separated. My mom and Mark moved to a rental house on the other side of Beyer, on a broad residential street called Boyce Avenue. I felt sorry that Mark had to go through all of that upheaval again— and all alone. However, he and mom both seemed to be doing well. Mom immersed herself in New Age literature and Eastern thought; she had not been to a United Methodist church in years. She now practiced yoga daily and read books by Tibetan monks and Hindu meditation masters, sharing discoveries along the way. She had an insatiable appetite for spiritual growth, grasping at everything as though knowledge could not come fast enough. An explorer blazing trails through a spiritual wilderness, she tossed tidbits of knowledge over her shoulder to me and Mark as if they were buried treasure. As for Guy, I had no doubt that he would be just fine. He was a tough old man; I called him occasionally to check in. He was, if not chipper, at least as buoyant as ever. My mom had been his fifth wife; he'd been through this kind of thing before.

In San Antonio, Michael insisted on dropping me off and picking me up for school every day, even though it was close by, because the roads I had to cross were major thoroughfares with a lot of traffic, and the only shortcut was over a steep, wooded hill that, at the time, was somewhat isolated. Every morning (that is, after the first morning, when he could hardly breathe for his anxiety on my behalf), he insisted that I read the highlights from the *San Antonio Express-News* out loud. He believed that I ought to know what was happening in the world, and asked me questions about the articles. That little ritual took up most of the brief trip to the school—and then it was off to another day.

I grew to love Incarnate Word. I enjoyed the challenge and variety of the modular classes, a deliberate schedule design that simulated college courses. Even sports were more fun. Beyer's sheer immensity made teams very competitive, but limited the options to learn new sports. At Incarnate Word, the girls played whatever they liked to . . . because they enjoyed it. A novel concept! This school culture was what I had been wanting. I joined the cross-country team—I wasn't a good runner, but wanted to learn how to run better. My dad, always admiring physical fitness, respected the cross-country instructor, Coach Nalepa, and loved going to the races to cheer for my team. He adopted an amused tone of voice when he talked about me and my teammates, calling us "the little shamrocks," as though we were his tiny vulnerable pets to protect and cherish.

Michael and I experienced a bumpy adjustment period, getting used to each other and developing a routine. We spent hours together and talked a lot, but normally about his job or my schoolwork. I didn't develop a deep understanding of what he liked or what made him tick, beyond that he was social and had an obvious penchant for the unusual. We both had strong independent streaks and I didn't drop anchor in the bay of his life. I floated a bit off the coastline, catching glimpses of the land. The tender inhabitants of his heart—the ones that shared secrets and dreams—did not speak to me. I don't know why I didn't feel more attached to him. Maybe he thought he had to remain aloof to parent, or he didn't know how to connect, or perhaps something was broken and sprung within me. He remained largely a mystery to me, but that fact prompted me to look outward more often, to lean into life and people, eyes wide, searching for common loves and understanding. One thing was certain: Life was different with Michael.

He surprised me a few weeks into the school year. After making some inquiries at Incarnate Word, Michael ferreted out how and where the initials on the plaid ties were done. He presented me with two little ties, all prim and neatly embroidered, at the end of September. My initials were displayed on one side and my class year on the other. Fortunately, I had mastered the knot by then. While visiting the school to pay tuition soon thereafter, he bought a bumper sticker for his truck that read, *I Love Shamrocks!* I was unaware of it until I saw it on the passenger's side of the Yukon as we headed to school one day.

One day, the government teacher, Mr. Gonzalez, who was popular with all of the girls because of his humor (not to mention his striking resemblance to George Clooney), inadvertently created a nickname for me that stuck. After I helped a shy fellow student earn points in a game, Mr. Gonzalez, as he turned to the board to increase her tally, muttered, "Eh, California's got your back."

The class laughed; even the shy girl looked at me and grinned.

From that day on, Mr. Gonzales always called me "California." For some reason, Michael thought that nickname was very amusing. He chuckled when I told him, and occasionally called me "Miss California" after that, like a pageant winner. That made me laugh.

Soon thereafter, he bought a string of bright shamrock lights for my room and made me a green crown from some St. Patrick's Day–themed wire. He grinned as he tucked the shamrocks in around a particularly unruly curl.

THE BURN UNIT AND THOMAS JEFFERSON

Michael worked at a hospital called Brooke Army Medical Center (BAMC) on Fort Sam Houston. He was a psychiatric nurse who worked with burn patients who had sustained some of the most horrendous injuries and disfigurement imaginable. He'd worked in the unit during his last years of active-duty service. Now that he was retired from the army, he assisted with a grant to re-search the long-term recovery prospects of burn patients: men and women, soldiers from war zones and all over the United States, who arrived to receive some of the best available care for burn injuries. It was the only center of its kind in the United States Defense Department.

BAMC was the major hospital on Fort Sam and occupied a huge new building, a state-of-the-art facility that presided over the surrounding landscape and nearby highways. The burn unit was on the fourth floor. We had only one vehicle, the Yukon, so Michael was often inconvenienced, leaving work to pick me up at the high school, only to return to the office to finish up some projects. I didn't like being stuck at the house, so it was easier to just go back to the office with him.

Occasionally we met some of his colleagues in the halls, but Michael rarely allowed me to go with him through the sections where the patients rested. When he did invite me, one impression about those quiet sections stuck with me throughout the years: The nurses spoke softly and the lights were very dim. One day when I was with him, I caught a glimpse of a burn patient in one of the private rooms, prone and completely still. Sunlight filtered through the window, and I understood just how badly these patients had been hurt. He—or she—looked like an empty, lifeless body, waiting for the touch of God. I realized how hard it would be to work in the burn unit amid that pain—those shattered and changed lives—every single day.

I stayed in Michael's office most of the time when I was at BAMC. It had a distinctive door, recognizable from all the way down the long and empty corridors of the building: Michael kept it covered in newspaper clippings. He taped headlines and meaningful stories all over the brown wooden door, and kept them there for months. Unfortunately, a lot of them were tragic stories, and not just about burn victims, so I tended to look the other way as I entered. I did not want to see the sad stories, and I thought it was a little weird that he displayed them that way.

Inside, the office was nothing like the lonely corridors where the patients recovered. It was a large and quiet room with standard-issue government furniture and wall cabinets—but it was full of toys. Most were themed sets made by a company called Playmobil. They included tiny movable figurines with horse and dog companions, miniature chairs, and small houses. I asked Michael about them once as he gathered paperwork for a meeting.

"One day a small family came by and I didn't have anything for the kids to play with," he replied. "I swore I'd never be caught unprepared like that again, not when so many of them have just gone through such a terrible time or suffered a loss like they have. I started collecting the sets for all of the kids in patients' families to play with, and after a while people just started donating to me. They knew I had toys in my office, and somebody would say, 'Hey, my kids don't play with this anymore,' or, 'I had these in my closets. . . .'"

His office became the go-to place for toys in the unit—for the children of both patients and colleagues. As a result, the overall effect was of a standard agency workspace that had collided with a day care.

I studied in his office many evenings, amid the toys, while he worked. BAMC provided a much-needed change of scenery for me, and the silence of the offices and clinics rivaled any library. There were several times when, my brain fried from memorizing

Latin verbs, I sat cross-legged on the floor and played with the toys like a kid myself. One time, I opened a drawer of his office cabinets and found not files—but three brand-new boxes of Playmobil sets.

Michael seemed to enjoy my company in the office; he often stopped by between patient interviews to check in, and when he wrapped up, we'd walk down the broad halls together, discussing where to go for dinner or what to do that evening.

❧

On calm evenings, when Michael and I both felt relaxed and didn't have work to do, we often took time to walk alongside the river, or sometimes just drove around San Antonio together, listening to music. The freeways of San Antonio were mercifully clear of congestion most of the time, and both of us often found the hum of the radio, the gentle lull of the road, and each other's company to comprise a perfect evening.

Michael was finicky; he occasionally got annoyed with little things, like a delay at the grocery store. Fortunately, genuine anger was rare with him, and the Mardi Gras highway incident was the only time I consciously remember seeing him out of control. That was comforting to me, because any form of anger or annoyance from him made me feel like we were strangers again. I didn't know what he would do and didn't rest comfortably in the idea that he would still love me. I was afraid that if I did something he really disliked, he would abandon me—leave me to myself and my own inadequate devices.

But those evenings with him were great—peaceful and free. Our harmony on those nights amazed me. I felt as if a part of myself had been frozen and still all of these years—because there was no resonance with the outside world, no link of validation and acceptance—and now it was finally warm under the rays of the sun. And I didn't realize it at the time, but it was because of him. With my mom, I had expressed one part of my personality, and with my dad I finally expressed another. For the first time I saw that just because my mom or brother might think something was weird didn't mean it *was* weird; there was another way—maybe millions of ways—of approaching life and defining myself. At times like that, I believed anything was possible, that I could go anywhere and do anything—not because life was necessarily better with my dad, but because suddenly I felt richer, more empowered, in my own heart. He made me see things another way, and that alone made me feel better: It was okay to be different.

It was during one of our evening drives that Michael confided that his favorite quote was from Thomas Jefferson and inscribed on the Jefferson Memorial in Washington, D.C. He closed his eyes for a moment when he recited the quote, as if lifting himself to a higher place—somewhere he wanted to live—"I have sworn upon the altar of God eternal hostility against every form of tyranny over the mind of man."

I smiled and repeated the words, trying to get them right. It was perfect. I could see why he liked it so much. It had become apparent to me, since moving to San Antonio, that Michael really appreciated the unusual and offbeat in life—not for shock value, but because of his intrinsic broad acceptance of others. That in society which forced people into stereotypes and tidy boxes galled him; the unexpected and surprising inspired him. His originality wasn't flashy. He expressed himself and validated others in an understated way. In the same manner that a pair of oxen might till a field, he gleefully eroded preconceived notions of "right" or "appropriate" in tiny, daily ways, like wearing a loud, colorful tie into a solemn work discussion. He delighted, in fact, in bucking convention; the "tyranny of the mind" was an enemy, it appeared, he engaged every day.

On one of our excursions together, while walking in Brackenridge Park, a city park near his house, we stopped at a café called Madhatters. It was in a secluded place, just off a tiny street known as Avenue B, a street so small it was not even on some maps. The restaurant was painted unconventionally in bright colors and covered in whimsical decor. Nothing matched. Plates, mugs, and utensils all looked like they might have come from a variety of kitchens throughout the world. The food was fantastic. I quickly found a favorite dish: the marvelous orange-cranberry scone. Often it would be served on a delicate china dinner plate with a gracious and feminine design, while the tiny serving cup was made of a thick ceramic and painted wild colors, like purple or orange. Michael, always a fan of the quirky and nonsensical, enjoyed a Madhatters café table as much as I did. The first time we went and saw the full dinner spread, he exclaimed, laughing, "This is wacky!" As soon as I heard the word "wacky," I knew that he was having a good time. (He said the same thing at a Weird Al Yankovic concert at Trinity University later that year.)

Michael quickly realized that I loved Madhatters, and it became part of the regular routine. I always ordered that treasured little scone and perhaps a hot chocolate. He brought his newspaper and sometimes got a slice of cake. We passed hours together. Every now and then he would lean back and smile, genuinely content. I liked it when he did that. There was something very rare and important about it. Michael didn't laugh deeply or totally relax often, but when he did it was incredibly *beautiful*. One time when he leaned back in his chair, so content, I looked at him and felt a surprising rush of love and admiration that culminated in a hard, heartfelt ball of personal will: *God, I want to remember this moment forever.*

LIGHT THE WAY

The University of the Incarnate Word (UIW) was across the street from Michael's modest home, and the mother school to my high school. Its campus abuts several major traffic intersections, but a long, low brick wall and a magnificent array of old oak trees diffuse the tension and noise from the city streets. The large, heavy limbs hang suspended over the asphalt of the city and the grass of the campus, a front line of serenity branching outward from the redbrick buildings of the university itself.

Michael loved the UIW campus. He shared and marveled at so many obscure facts related to it and the nearby Brackenridge Park that, as before with anyplace he had ever moved, I wondered how on earth he found the time to research it all. The headwaters of the San Antonio River well up from a spring located on and around the UIW campus, and he took me to see it. As we watched the water flow, he exclaimed with humor and silly glee, "Look at the baby river!"

For Christmas, he informed me one day, UIW lit up the entire campus in Christmas lights in an annual festival called Light the Way. The regional H-E-B supermarket chain generously donated money to cover the university's larger electricity bill generated by all of the Christmas wattage. Michael loved being involved in community projects and special occasions, and he was very excited about this event.

I, on the other hand, was more private and less confident. I hesitated about being a volunteer, attendee, or active participant in social things—and tried to avoid them whenever possible. I often experienced drastic internal conflict between reckless courage and painful caution, sometimes seesawing between both in a split second. However, if I wanted something badly, boldness normally won out. Everything was unleashed in pursuit of the goal. Despite the fact that I made decisions that some might attribute to confidence—like moving to San Antonio—I believed them to be more the result of desperation. In those cases, I had to do *something*. When I didn't feel pressure, though, I did not seek out the new and unknown.

Michael's natural enthusiasm, however, was like a California wave that tumbled over me and carried me along on whatever idea he had set his sights upon. Throughout the autumn, he had rebuttals for my grumblings about being obligated to socialize with strangers at volunteer and social functions; he told me in no uncertain terms that on occasion I was just plain silly. Sometimes he would simply announce, "Get your shoes on. We're going out."

He was completely right. But without him around to drag me out the door, it simply would not have happened. I would have been content at home with a good book and a breeze coming through the window. The constant exposure to novel things and new people created a budding confidence in me. I never had a bad time with him. The tiny social successes accumulated and I began to perk up a bit, to be less reserved and worried about other people's reactions.

"So . . . would you like to go to the lighting ceremony?" he asked me near Christmastime.

I loved sleeping under Christmas trees while I was growing up, and I'd never seen a whole campus lit up in lights. Out of simple childish delight, and for once mercifully unhampered by gross teenage insecurities, I answered, "Yeah!"

We went together. Shadows and soft murmurs filled the campus. People milled about speaking in low tones, and then suddenly someone flipped the switch. The campus was transformed into a magical wonderland of twinkling lights. My dad, high on the lights and the night, chatted with people passing by. I remained quiet, just soaking up the colors and listening to the far-off laughter. *This is awesome!* My dad patted me on the back, interrupting my reverie.

"You know, Tiffany, it would be very cool if you went to college here at UIW. It's such a pretty campus, and you're already at the high school."

Oh, my God. My heart plummeted in my chest.

College.

⌁

A few weeks later, my dad suggested going downtown to watch the New Year's fireworks display at the Tower of the Americas for the new millennium—the year 2000. He wanted it to be special—an *event*. My quiet and less outgoing style—the book and the breeze—would have to wait for another New Year, but that was okay: I was starting to outgrow that approach.

The Tower of the Americas, the centerpiece of New Year's festivities in San Antonio, is a large structure that looks rather like a giant cattail, or a campfire stick with a really roasted, brown marshmallow on the top. The "marshmallow" is in fact a restaurant, and apparently good, but for all the majesty of the location—rotating way above the city—I had never been. Nor, honestly, did I ever feel the desire to go. It was enough that the marshmallow was in the sky—I did not need to be inside of it to appreciate it. I found the Tower of the Americas to be a comforting landmark, the first structure of the familiar downtown cluster. On long days or long drives, it was reassuring to see. It meant that I was close to home.

On New Year's Eve, Michael and I managed to find a spot among a large crowd right on the rail of the highest level of a downtown parking garage, which was one of the best places to see the fireworks. Strangers gathered near us, all excited. There was a feeling of unity, of sudden comrades celebrating together. The rooftop of the garage was open to the cool night sky studded with stars, and all of us stood together at the railing, marveling at the beauty, waiting in anticipation. Michael turned to me, beaming, before the fireworks began and said, "I'm so happy to be here with you. I wish Mark could be here too. But this is so good."

I knew he missed Mark. Sometimes I believed he must be disappointed that he just got me for a while. He never acted disappointed with circumstances; he only noted Mark's absence on occasion. However, in those small comments, I sensed a vast untold story; as if a foreign coup had been summed up in seven words on a tabloid.

He paused a moment and looked up at the sky. Then he repeated softly, in awe and mostly to himself, "This is so good." His tone of voice was calm and pleasant, almost dreamy. I looked around, trying to see the world with his eyes and appreciate the moment for all of the reasons that it was so good.

Moments later—with a crashing sound and a flash of rainbow light—the New Year, the new century, and the new millennium arrived together in one radiant moment. Time stopped—and passed—in moments, in rhythm with the sky bursts, until the fireworks exploded into a marvelous, unsustainable crescendo that then, ever so slowly, died away into the night.

"I love you, Tiffany!" My father leaned forward and gave me a hug.

"I love you too, Dad." I hugged him tightly, wishing Mark and Mom could have been here too.

We let go and exchanged "Happy New Year!" wishes and big grins with everybody nearby. I hoped this landmark New Year was a good omen.

Unbeknownst to my dad, I had recently sent out my first college application.

GRADUATION

Ever since my sophomore year of high school, I had received promotional materials from colleges, everything from low-budget flyers to full-color brochures, announcing the benefits of attending different schools. With the sensory overload, I stopped paying attention. I ignored the junk mail and, with the confidence of someone who didn't actually have to face a decision yet, indulged in the smug feeling of being desperately sought and unwilling to be won. But the truth was, I was scared about applying for college and didn't want to think about it.

Toward the end of the school year, I won some recognition on the National Latin Exam. I was shocked, and Sister Mary was downright delighted. A few days later, my classmates voted me "Most Likely to Hold a Seat in Congress." Again, I was surprised, but primarily because I'd never heard of such a peculiar, specific category. When Michael heard about it, he was thrilled. He even called Madhatters that night and reserved an orange-cranberry scone under his name for me. He didn't want them to be out when he brought me to celebrate.

I thought his gesture was one of the sweetest things I had ever heard. But I felt horrible, eaten from within by ravenous anxiety—about the future, an education, a career. I was too worried about college to be concerned about Congress. Others' idea of my destiny was far more positive than my own appraisal. The past few weeks had been grueling. My classmates appeared excited about college, throwing out privileged names and getting acceptance letters. Some had already purchased college sweatshirts, as if they could paste themselves into their desired future. I, on the other hand, felt almost embarrassed about trying. Fear of failure tormented me. I withdrew again, seeking refuge in my insecure shell.

My parents—both of them—tried to support me, but, not knowing what I needed (namely, hand-holding), were unable to offer vital assistance. I didn't know how to ask for help, so I answered their persistent inquiries with vague assertions. I made a show of mentioning college names and my diligent effort—an effort that was, in fact, a bumbling and haphazard mess.

I felt overwhelmed, as if every student in the United States needed her own review board if she were to plan her future properly. I applied to a college in the Northeast just because someone I admired attended. I thought it was worth a try. I worked hard, clandestinely, on the application, pouring creativity into it. I suffered and worried in silence, every moment weakening my confidence. But I didn't know what else to do. I sent out a couple other applications to colleges in Texas. Every decision felt like a skyscraper—and life an increasingly stormy sea. I threw out college applications like spitballs against the wall of destiny, hoping one would stick.

Then one day, a letter came in the mail.

It was from the college in the Northeast.

My dad wasn't home yet. I grabbed the letter and ran to my room, glancing furtively at Mary's alcove as I slipped the letter under the bed. I couldn't bear to look at it yet—acceptance or refusal. Michael would be coming home any second, and I wanted to be calm.

Late that night, after we had dinner and he'd gone to bed in the front bedroom, I quietly padded to my bedroom and took the letter out. Sitting on the soft flannel sheets in front of the warm glow of the space heater, I opened it up and, taking a breath, read two words:

"We regret . . ."

I didn't read any more. There was no need. No doubt a smart individual, or likely a whole committee of them, spent hours getting the collegial turns of phrase just right to crush someone's dreams in the nicest way possible. But it would deliver the equivalent of three words: No, thank you.

I went quietly into the bathroom as the heat of shame and embarrassment swept through me. It flooded me like a tide; I locked the door right before I collapsed in a miserable puddle on the floor. I cried quietly, determined not to wake my dad up in the next room, feeling like an utter failure, and wondering what I was going to do with my life.

Nobody wants me. What am I doing wrong?

Two days later, another letter arrived in the mail. From Texas A&M University.

Another rejection.

I hid it too. And got a tummyache.

❧

About two weeks later, a friend dropped me off at my house after school. I unlocked the front door and pushed it open slightly, surprised to feel resistance. I heard a slow grating sound, as if something were being pushed across the wood floor. Concerned that I was inadvertently breaking something, I peeked behind the half-open door to see what was making that noise. A large package sat squat, like a toad, against the other side.

That the postman managed to squish it through the mail slot astounded me. I pushed the door open and picked the brown package up as I walked into the house. Large packages normally came in for my dad; this one was addressed to me. The return address was "Texas A&M at Galveston." Just another promotional mailing, I thought. But a second glance and then intuition struck: No school would spend that much money on a package to send it to a *potential* student. This was an investment.

With some scissors, I cut through the thick manila paper and bubble wrap of the shipping envelope. Inside, there was a maroon T-shirt—and an acceptance letter.

I sat there, astounded. I could not comprehend the package—I didn't apply to that school.

But everything was there. They had all of my information perfectly correct: documentation to help me go to orientation at the campus, registration forms for living in the dorms. I sat on my bed with my brow furrowed, shifting the papers repeatedly, uselessly.

How did this happen?

I read through the acceptance letter again. I had applied to Texas A&M University at College Station (the main campus) and was rejected. But the main campus had a transfer program through the Galveston campus, a small maritime academy dedicated to ocean studies. If I did well in Galveston, after two years I could transfer into the main campus. It was something, but certainly not splendid; nor was I clear if it was standard procedure or a temporary special program. A maritime academy? On one hand, I felt like the dregs of the university's choices, but on the other . . . I was accepted into a college! Victory had arrived, of a sort.

My dad came home from work about twenty minutes later, and, still baffled myself but willing to accept the truth of it all, I shared the good news. He hadn't received any updates on my college applications beyond my casual and intentionally vague assertions that everything was fine; I'd never told him about the two rejection letters.

"That's *great* news! I'm so proud of you!"

Proud of me? I thought. *This feels like an accident!* I showed him the particulars of the acceptance, but felt like I was trying to convince myself that it was real. As he looked through the stuff with me, he asked, "What are you going to study there until you transfer?"

"I'm not sure. They only have a few majors, it looks like, and most of them are science. Maritime administration sounds good. . . ."

"Business?"

"Yeah."

"Perfect!"

I wanted to make this work. I'd been miraculously snatched from the jaws of lifelong failure, offered a chance at redemption. The thought of transferring midway through college had never occurred to me as even possible.

"You might even want to stick with that one for all four years. If you transfer in the middle, it might delay your graduation," Michael went on. "That's how some people go to college for years and years and never get a degree. Even if it ends up being something that you don't want to do, at least you'll have a degree."

I saw the wisdom of his point. I determined then and there that, whatever degree I pursued, I would stick it out until the end. He seemed to understand the potential pitfalls of certain circumstances, even if I felt he didn't always understand me; his advice carried significant weight. Still feeling shell-shocked by my future appearing in such an unexpected fashion, as if space junk had landed in my yard, I started to recover and think of practical matters—that was my strong suit. The registration forms, dormitory paperwork, and even the prospect of sharing the news with family and friends energized me. Michael, in the meantime, took off his tie and changed his shoes. Then he grinned and said, "Here, get your shoes on. Let's go out and celebrate!"

As he tied his shoes, he asked, "What's the mascot?"

"Uh . . ." I pulled the package out again. "It's a Sea Aggie. . . ."

Michael laughed heartily. "A Sea Aggie! Oh, that's cute!"

❧

On May 21, I graduated with the Class of 2000 at Incarnate Word High School. Shamrocks were everywhere: on the graduation program; on the shirts of some attendees; on barrettes, ribbons, and jewelry throughout the large building. My mom and Mark flew in from California for the ceremony, and all of my new friends were there. Heidi, a good friend who admitted she had a covert crush on my dad, stopped by to say hello before the ceremony. She made a special point of acknowledging him and gave me the toothy smile of a tiger on the prowl. I pretended not to notice.

The principal and several of the senior instructors were on the stage to hand out the diplomas to the graduates. I was uncomfortably self-conscious and eager to get the ridiculous green gown off as soon as the ceremony was over. This was not my thing: the ritual, the attention. Everyone expected the graduates to be happy, but I just sat still and tried to make it through.

My name was called. I got up, tried not to trip, and wanted to disappear. I was conscious of the steps . . . the stage . . . a hand. Mr. Gonzalez was handing me the diploma. We made eye contact and he grinned, all teeth and happiness. It was contagious: This *was* a big moment!

He grasped my hand tightly and said, "Good job, California!"

A wave of intense affection and admiration for him took me by surprise. *Oh, thank you, sir! George Clooney is lucky to look like you!* My mom and brother were smiling in the bleachers. And my dad was radiant. I thought he stood even a little taller than usual. I suddenly felt proud.

Afterward, Michael laughed. "Time to get ready, Sea Aggie!"

I-10, EASTBOUND

Galveston is a barrier island, long and narrow, off the coast of Texas. A large causeway leads to it, an intimidating bridge that spans high above the water channel and provides an unmitigated view of the heavy industry and shipping lanes in the area.

When I started at Texas A&M at Galveston in the fall, the college had only three thousand students enrolled. The campus is on a tiny landmass near Galveston called Pelican Island, a man-made island comprised entirely of ship channel dredging and connected to the mainland by a drawbridge notorious for often getting stuck in midair. A huge concentration of chemical plants line the only car-accessible route to the island, and defined my first impression of my new college home. The drive in was dominated by gray factories spewing smoke for miles, and prompted only one thought: *Why would Texas A&M build a campus here? This place just looks like Houston's toilet!*

Michael had moved me into the new dorm room and bought necessities for my first semester from the Post Exchange on Fort Sam, including colorful twin-size bedding for my dorm room. Mom sent care packages throughout the semester full of my favorite baked pastries, tiny comic strips cut from newspapers, and occasionally a new book she thought I would enjoy. One of the packages had a Chinese box in it. The box was a game or oracle called the "I Ching." Apparently you could rub some sticks together, ask a question, and then the sticks (with the help of a book) gave you an answer. I tried it a few times and it provided surprisingly accurate answers.

The newfound freedom of college dizzied me. The first few nights I was wild. It was completely novel to me that I could hang out with friends and drink liquor into the wee hours with no one to tell me what to do. But the classes soon demanded more of my time. I was naturally responsible, and drinking made me feel sluggish, so I steadied. I started to meditate a little bit every now and then—to be more calm and centered. I figured out what I could handle in the balance of recreation, socializing, and academics, and I harmonized with the rhythm of Galveston. The days were relaxed, full of breezes and hot sunshine. I normally found it easy to ignore the presence of the nearby factories and industry, especially on the gulf side of the island. The local population almost doubled in size every workday as the two largest employers on the island, American National Insurance Company and the University of Texas Medical Branch (UTMB), filled their offices. The hustle and bustle of the morning and afternoon commutes were the only citylike events that Galveston experienced. The rest of the time, it had the slow pace and casual attitude typical of island living. Galveston wasn't a global heavyweight; it was a place where Texans and visitors alike sat back and enjoyed the slow, enduring strength of Texas.

For a college student with textbooks to read and studying to do, the beach town was surprisingly ideal. The road grid of Galveston was simple: Streets that ran roughly north–south were numbered; streets that ran east–west were lettered; and occasionally there was a thoroughfare with a common or landmark name. The road trio of Broadway, Seawall, and Harborside became the triangle around which I lived my college life; the familiar signs felt comforting. I discovered new things constantly, even on blocks driven dozens of times: a mansion tucked behind some large trees, or a modest bungalow that had seen better days.

꩜

After my initial blowout, I avoided the hard partiers, but also the overly studious types—extremism feels imbalanced to me. I sensed a danger in that regard and ran the middle ground at school, sometimes spending time in the library just reading books that had nothing to do with my college coursework, or playing soccer with my friends. I did okay, but unfortunately watched some of my new friends make bad decisions that first year—several dropped out of college completely.

My communication with Michael was not as strong as it had been when we lived together. For my part, I was focused on my academic work amid all of the new, magnetic distractions around campus, and the simple fact that we didn't see each other every day prevented the kind of familiarity we'd achieved in San Antonio. So much of our togetherness was rooted in being in close quarters every day: going out for dinner and sharing observations. We simply weren't physically close anymore. The budding sense of camaraderie that made me smile slowly evaporated. I was pretty much, it seemed, on my own again. His e-mails and calls got shorter. He was busy, he loved me very much, but he had to go now.

He also had a new girlfriend, a woman named Beth. I'd met her only briefly a couple of times during trips back, but they had been dating since shortly after I left San Antonio. From the little I gathered, Beth was very social, devoutly Christian, and had a creative streak. Michael obviously admired her originality and faith, and appeared happy to sit back and bask in her lively presence. He seemed to have forgotten me. I knew that wasn't the case, but it *felt* like that. He referred to her house as "the house on Magnolia" or just "Magnolia," and he had been spending a lot more time at Magnolia recently. I was happy for him, but he seemed far more distant. The old feeling from when I was a kid came back. He seemed generous whenever we were together—with affection, with money, with all things—but he was not easy to approach when we were apart.

He sometimes stopped by Galveston on the way from San Antonio to see his dad, my Grandpa Yates, in Slidell, Louisiana—and then again on the way back. He didn't carry a cell phone, so getting in touch with him during the trips wasn't easy; he would call at his discretion, or just meet me somewhere at an appointed time. His visits felt like an old acquaintance was passing through town, or an executive was stopping by to see how a branch office was doing. He always took me out grocery shopping, and often took my friends and me out to dinner. Together we found some restaurants that eventually became favorites, like the Spot on Seawall, which he loved for its burgers and chocolate milk shakes. His short visits were pleasant but infrequent. But his presence was always in the background—a constant in brief e-mails and phone calls—and I knew that I could call him if I got into trouble.

Well, I got into some trouble.

It started innocuously: I saw this guy for the first time in the university cafeteria one quiet evening. Immediately after a workout, I rushed in to grab some food before the cafeteria closed. He sat all by himself at a table near the meal line, looking sad and lonely. His muscular body slouched at the table, as if he were tired of life, and his blond head hung low over his dinner.

"Well, hello," I said, just trying to be supportive and cheerful. "How are you?"

He looked up with piercing eyes; they delved straight into mine. He was anything but tired of life. His powerful physique suddenly looked commanding, as if he were, at the moment, immediately alert and ready to change all of existence around him—bodily. The sense of resolute power took my breath away; I had never met a man so intense. When his eyes met mine, his gaze felt overwhelmingly magnetic. Suddenly I could not get enough oxygen. I didn't know one person could have such an instant attraction to another human being.

Eyes widening, he relaxed into the chair. "Better now!" he replied. He watched me pass by, his eyes way more than friendly.

And that was it. I couldn't stop thinking about him. His masculine presence, concentrated and instinctive, was arrestingly sexy. He was obviously older, but felt to me like a mythical hero, powerful in a natural way, like a lion in Africa. Even if he was silent, people could *feel* him in the room. He looked like a warrior-king, a man who could get things done—and quickly.

I was smitten.

Fortunately, in a crowd of freshmen, one could ask questions about someone without generating interest. Everyone, after all, was new. I took advantage of the situation as best I could to gather intel about this compelling man like a one-girl government agency. I found out via my classmate that he was a new student there and, to top it off, an ex–Navy SEAL.

A couple weeks later, I ran into the man himself on the broad sidewalk that bisected the eastern part of campus. We walked in opposite directions, each of us with friends, but our companions started talking to each other when we passed. Seeing the opportunity at hand, with him served up before me like a luscious piece of cake, I spoke up: "I think I've seen you around. My name is Tiffany. . . ." I extended my hand. "What's yours?"

He said his name, but all I registered was his body language: He leaned forward in that broad-motion way men sometimes do when they're eager, when they've been waiting to see someone. His enthusiasm surprised me—I hadn't expected reciprocity, but felt overjoyed to see it! My mind skidded to a stop when I realized I hadn't understood what he said. "I'm sorry. I didn't catch that. What is your name?"

He pronounced the single syllable slowly and more clearly, obviously accustomed to having to repeat it: "Fox."

I said it, letting the name settle in my mind, and smiled broadly at him. *How perfectly unusual!* The friends finished talking; Fox was watching me. I determined to play it cool and indifferent, which, while risky, was, I'd found, normally more effective with guys than coming on too strong. With an attitude of self-sufficiency, as if I didn't want or need anything from him, I pivoted to leave, and called over my shoulder as I threw a cursory wave, "Take care, Fox. See you around!"

❧

Later that semester, Dad called with some bizarre news: He was running for mayor of San Antonio.

I was stunned. I encouraged and supported him—profusely so—but later, after I had time to think about it, I felt sickeningly apprehensive on his behalf. *He practically just moved there. He doesn't know the power brokers, and he's not established in the community.* My quick evaluation concluded in a dead end of realistic prospects: He didn't stand a chance of winning.

I felt fiercely protective of him. I cringed inside at the possible scenarios that might break his heart. But I felt intensely proud of his courage and pluck. That was pretty amazing: to just move to a large city and run for mayor.

While Michael worked and campaigned in San Antonio, I burned the candle at both ends in Galveston. The next semester, Fox and I had a class together and started seeing each other. I was busy: studying, hanging out with friends, and trying to get a grip on who the heck I was. Toward the end of my freshman year, I decided to date Fox exclusively. I adored him.

Unfortunately, my idea of Special Forces and the reality of dating a man who had been in Special Forces were two *very* different things. When my dad found out that Fox and I were dating seriously, he was quiet and didn't appear pleased. He had met Fox briefly at school one afternoon; I could tell immediately that he wasn't impressed. With people he liked, Michael asked a lot of questions; with Fox that afternoon, he did not. Fox had been a little theatrical, trying to impress and win my dad over, but there was too much loud laughter and bravado. Michael was able, and normally happy, to chat with anybody, but his silence was a sign that he was either not comfortable or not pleased. I gathered there was something about Fox that provoked him, but I didn't know what it was. His lack of approval made me somewhat apprehensive, as Michael was extremely intelligent and perceptive; however, since he didn't say anything negative outright about Fox, I had nothing but vague impressions to consider.

With Michael, I had to infer a lot. He did not often communicate when it came to personal matters, and sometimes my skill was not refined enough. I lacked sufficient knowledge, insight, or maturity. How he felt about dating and romance—with regard to himself or anyone else, including me—I never did quite grasp, although I do remember one time he told me, "Don't let the boys dazzle you with their charms!" I knew that he was extremely private about his own personal life. In fifteen years, I had met only three of his girlfriends (including Beth), although I gathered, from various letters in the box room and innuendos in conversation, that he had had many.

Michael cautioned me vaguely about Fox—nothing specific, just a suggestion of disapproval and wariness. But he never dictated to me or told me what to do. He must have known it wouldn't have done any good. I liked Fox. As I got to know him, he proved to be astoundingly intelligent and perceptive, and there was a profound unspoken resonance between the two of us. The only issue was that he was a little unpredictable, as if there were a fire within him that at any point might start to rage out of control. He was wild, but I thought it was in a manly and noble way. I thought that, after all that he had been through—the rigorous training, actual missions, and the intense psychological pressure of the SEAL teams—he had earned by blood and sweat the self-awareness and discipline to make the right choices. He was a little paranoid, but I thought it was understandable, given what he'd seen and done. He, in general, appeared to be protective and patriotic. However, as many people know—but few fully appreciate—appearances can be deceiving, and my ex–Navy SEAL was about to introduce me to the darker side of life.

❦

In San Antonio, there were a lot of candidates for mayor that year. Michael didn't win. I had been a little ambivalent about the scrutiny that might come from being the daughter of the mayor anyway. But I was ecstatic when I heard that he actually earned some votes! Four hundred and forty people voted for him. I loved them all. He said to me a few days after the results were announced, "I didn't think that I would actually win, but there was that possibility. It has been a wacky ride. I've met some amazing people—really great people who believe in making the world a better place."

I felt immensely proud of him, and congratulated him repeatedly. After I hung up, I closed my eyes. It helped me, when experiencing deep feelings (good or bad), to meditate and be quiet for a while. Right then, gratitude swelled within me. I visualized all of those voters in San Antonio, all of those precious people who supported my dad. I imagined them as bright little stars walking around the city. In my mind, they were sprinkled about Bexar County, twinkling. I sent them waves of gratitude—for voting in general, for voting for him in particular, for being who they were. After visualizing that for a while, I thought, *Well, that's not cool to think that voters who vote for my dad are the only ones worthwhile* . . . so I had all of the voters twinkling . . . and then: *Well, shoot, I can't just stop at voters*, so it was everybody in San Antonio . . . and, *San Antonio isn't the only city with cool people.* Before long the whole world was lit up in my mind like a holiday ornament in the sky, and I found myself grinning to think of the world in such a way.

A few weeks later, when my dad was in Galveston, he took me to the Spot to have burgers and milk shakes. I had been dating Fox for about two months at this point; Michael and I were talking seriously about relationships, and about Fox in particular.

My dad leaned forward. "Tiff, why do you like Fox?"

I considered his question thoughtfully. "I like the fact that he does his own thing. He understands me better than anyone else I've ever met. I feel like he gets me." I glanced up at the ceiling and—looking back to my dad—decided to refrain from mentioning that I also thought Fox was *hot*.

"Well, I'm glad for that. That's important. It's nice to feel understood. But here's something important to keep in mind: You get to know a person by their behavior, not what they say. Little things mean a lot. Respect is in all of those little things. Respect is when a person listens to you, makes time for you, and stands up for you. And vice versa. You need to listen, make time, and stand up for your friends. People are always giving signs about whether they are good or bad. Bad behavior is like a red flag. It could be simple, like a rude tone of voice. Or it could be worse, like violence. You know—in your heart—when something is wrong. You should make a note of it. Remember it. These are all red flags that point to a destructive person who is disrespectful and could be dangerous. All I'd like you to do is watch out. Watch out for red flags. The more there are, the less you should hang out with that person. Okay?"

"Okay," I replied solemnly. His words struck me as good advice, but while I appreciated that he was speaking so earnestly to me, I didn't think any of it actually applied to Fox. If Michael had worries, they just sprang from the overactive imagination of a dad, the same irrational fears that might plague any parent. I tried to comfort him, to make him comprehend that I could make my own choices just fine.

I got home late that night and decided to consult the I Ching that my mom had sent me. A game or an oracle, I wasn't sure what it was exactly, but it had been so accurate that I thought it might be interesting to see what it had to say about Fox.

I pulled the I Ching out, laid the book to the side, and started rubbing the red plastic sticks together. They clattered like a horse-drawn carriage over cobblestones. I asked the I Ching whether my relationship with Fox was a good thing, and for any advice. Laying the sticks out on the carpet in front of me, I looked in the book for a description of the composite symbol that the red rods displayed. The style of writing always struck me as strange—full of rich imagery that resonated more with instinct and intuition than the logical mind—very unlike any American game or book I had ever seen. The sign that appeared was called *Chun*, represented by water over thunder, and otherwise known as "Difficulty at the Beginning." I read the description, and the last line haunted me well into the night: *Horse and wagon part. Bloody tears flow.*

THE LONG DARK HOURS OF THE NIGHT—I

I decided to take courses over the summer to get credits faster. School was excellent, but during that hot season, unpleasant little things started happening with Fox. He became impatient if I didn't respond to a call or e-mail, more terse if we disagreed on something, and in general displayed tiny disconnects in logical thought that appeared to be the result of emotional distress or a momentary lapse in concentration. I thought all of these minor variations were part of the process of getting to know someone; Malachi, after all, was the only person I'd actually dated "exclusively" for more than a week. This was all new to me. Wanting, as I did, to see the best in everyone, I made excuses for him:

He's just upset today, mad about that test.

He was just drunk last night, too much partying with his friends.

But one day there was a particularly nasty explosion on his part—completely irrational and unprovoked—and I actually laughed out loud as he ranted. All I could see in my mind's eye were dozens of mini-Dads around him, all waving red flags, and I couldn't help laughing.

I'd recently started to change what I said around Fox, to prevent him from getting mad. I edited myself—thinking it would suit him. Maybe that was part of getting along with somebody. I had adjusted myself and my normal reactions for years in small ways with my mom and Mark, after all, so they wouldn't think I was too weird or different. But then—and now—it frustrated me. Fox's unpredictable behavior was now a genuine problem, sometimes distracting me from my own responsibilities and obligations at school. I constantly wondered when he would get out of control or what he would do next.

Then, for whatever reason, things settled down with him. There was a long period of harmony at the start of my sophomore year, no flare-ups, temper tantrums, or strange lapses in understanding on Fox's part, and my hopes for the future expanded. I thought we were through the worst of it. All fronts—friends, school, and home—seemed relatively peaceful, happy, and harmonious.

Fox surprised me one day after he'd just returned from a trip to Florida; while there, he got his first tattoo.

"Wanna see it?" he asked.

"Of course!" I said.

He pulled the shirt fabric off of his shoulder and I gaped in shock. There, in bold lines on skin that was still pink from the tattooing procedure, were my initials, T.M.Y., in the traditional layout of the Texas A&M logo.

"Oh, my God." I gasped. I felt appalled—then flattered—and then aghast again. It seemed like such a reckless thing to do! I half wanted the tattoo to be a joke. I felt his skin gently. "Is it real?"

"Of course it's real!" he seemed slightly put-off, but still beamed.

"Wow, Fox!"

"Wow, Tiff!" He gave me a big hug. "I love you!"

"I love you too!" I still couldn't believe it. Part of me felt sick and another part elated. That someone could love me enough to do that was incredible; that someone would actually do it was disturbing.

The weeks passed and I tried to alternately forget and accept Fox's new tattoo. I finally felt like I was on the right path in life. Circumstances were so steady, and my time with Fox so rewarding and full of laughter, that the thought occurred to me, *I could marry him.*

In my head, traditional marriage was weak and flimsy; my belief in its permanency had been eroded by constant proof otherwise. Even so, I felt a deep need for a partner of some sort. It seemed to me that, however much the institution of marriage had been twisted and beaten by modern society into a walking farce, something of the legitimately valuable remained in the idea of commitment and partnership. I had, over the last few months, created a workable idea of marriage for myself. It was a positive venture—not a negative imprisonment, hard and black like my parents' reality—but more like an alliance of partners.

My idea of marriage required principles I had begun, through experience, to deeply value, including integrity, patience, and compassion. I believed that two people, armed with honesty and kindness, who mustered their forces together, in support of each other and for the good of all, really couldn't fail. The failures I had seen, I reasoned, had intrinsic, myriad flaws: deceit, selfish intentions, ignorance, or a lack of personal strength. I admired Fox. We understood each other. We worked well together. I wasn't looking for him to make me happy or trying to lean on him for support. What could go wrong? Not one to beat around the bush when I knew what I wanted, I asked him a few weeks later, "Hey, Fox, do you want to get married?"

᠆ᡃ᠆

In a cursory formality before the justice of the peace, with no real announcements to anyone beforehand, we got married.

My brother, Mark, just happened to be visiting from California that day, and attended the small ceremony in Galveston. My mom, miles away in California, was surprisingly silent. She sent me a simple message: *Congratulations on your marriage.* I realized from its brevity that I had inadvertently hurt my mom's feelings. I didn't mean to, and felt bad for disappointing her. I really and truly did not think that many people would be interested in attending; I didn't feel worthy of being the center of attention, didn't want to cause headaches and stress by spending money I didn't have for a celebration of myself and my new husband. And besides, the common elements of a wedding struck me at the time as self-absorbed and wasteful. The only way I could see having a wedding and it being a truly fun, meaningful event was for it to be a celebration of all the invitees—the special people in the couple's lives. If I were to do that, I would want it to be an incredible party full of gratitude and recognition that would have cost a fortune in time and money.

Lacking the resources for that kind of gala, I opted for next to nothing.

My dad was perplexed beyond belief. He visited a week later. While having lunch, he leaned forward, ignoring his food and favorite chocolate milk shake, and asked bluntly, "Why did you marry him?"

I shifted in my chair, oddly ashamed, as if I had to justify my decision to him. It was abundantly evident that he thought I'd made a mistake. "I don't know," I replied. "We love each other, and I think it can work."

"Tiffany, I really feel like you're just looking for a friend. You can have friends and not marry them."

I looked down at the table and frowned. *Dad doesn't understand at all!* I would be the first to admit that I didn't know what I was doing. But I loved Fox and wanted to take life as it came, side by side with him. Fox made me feel strong and hopeful. *He's lecturing me like he thinks I'm an idiot. He thinks I just need a friend? Does he think I don't have friends?*

But maybe my dad sensed something.

Fox changed entirely, and almost immediately, after we got married. He grew controlling; his language in general shifted from cooperative to demanding, and his behavior became more erratic, revolving around many late nights in a row at bars with friends. One night, I stayed at his apartment (we still had separate apartments because he had a couple weeks left on his lease), expecting him to be home any moment, and fell asleep after studying. He came home bleeding and belligerent in the middle of the night. When, sleepily rubbing my eyes, I asked him what happened, he said some guy attacked him on the walk home from the bar and he had to "show the guy that he'd made a mistake." I was shocked and full of questions: "Where were you? Why did you walk home from that bar?"—the one he cited was four miles away—"Did you call the police? Are you okay?"

He was a mess; less than half of the things he said made sense. I gaped at him. Life with Fox was not off to a great start. I was about to learn a sharp lesson by ignoring all of the red flags along the way: Violence as a profession and drinking as a hobby do not make a hero.

❧

In the middle of March—about two weeks after he came home in the middle of the night and a month after we'd gotten married—I went to Fox's apartment after studying to have dinner and hang out. It was his last night in the place. He seemed calm and content at first, and I thought everything was fine.

But then, out of the blue, he started acting aggressive and physical. There was no trigger event that I could identify. We weren't arguing; everything was peaceful. In a heartbeat, he just exited normal stage left. He suddenly behaved and appeared, in fact, completely insane. The look on his face was full of fury—as if he were angry—but behind his eyes there was no semblance of self-awareness that I could see. It was bloodcurdling. I don't remember everything, but at one point he shoved me against the wall and slammed my head into it several times. He asked, "Do you feel that?" I cowered, beside myself with confusion, and replied, pleadingly, "Y-yes, I do . . . please stop!" But he didn't. Even at the time, part of my mind was commenting in perfect, objective clarity: *Boy, that's a strange thing for him to ask. Of course I feel it when he beats my head against the wall.*

I tried to get away, but he barricaded me in the kitchen.

At the time, Fox probably weighed about one hundred pounds more than I did. I had never fought with anyone in my life, aside from minor bouts with my brother. I didn't even have, as anyone who saw me dance could attest, a strong concept of how to move my body in a coordinated effort. Fox, on the other hand, had trained for more than a decade in how to kill people. Every move that he made could maximize injury, pain, and damage in a sequence that would have looked, if it hadn't had been so morbid, like destructive ballet.

When Fox started moving toward me in that kitchen, I saw the end of my life. As the weight of the realization hit me, even amid the motion and drama of the moment, I had one thought: *No, I don't want to die! I want to tell Mom I love her one more time!* I no longer felt like I was in the room with a human being; I was in a room with a man possessed by a vicious demon, some entity that thrived on cruelty and another's pain. I couldn't comprehend how to interact with him—he literally did not appear to be thinking—and I didn't know how to put my will into events to change what was happening. He grabbed my right hand—I had hurt it playing catch with a football a couple days before. He knew that and started crushing it in his hands to make it hurt more.

It was incredibly painful—and absolutely crazy. I didn't understand any of it, and the abuse went on for nearly an hour. At some point, he grabbed my hair and flung me across the room. I felt my vertebrae crack and misalign in a terrible sound; I really thought that was the moment: I would die of a broken neck.

Then, sometime later—it could have been seconds or minutes or aeons—something happened and Fox backed away from me—he shook his head and, for a moment, the light of humanity came into his eyes. He looked like he was trying to control himself and said, "This is evil, this is evil," under his breath.

But the next second the man was gone and the brainless, muscled fiend was back—he was crazy again, and threw my luggage across the room.

At some point Fox had slowed his assault and I somehow escaped the apartment. I ran. I raced down the stairs as fast as I could. To this day, I have no idea how I got out of that apartment. The fresh air—I had never felt air so wonderfully refreshing—poured by my face. Carrying a small backpack and my keys, I practically launched myself into my car and peeled out of the parking lot.

Oh, my God! What the hell just happened?

I was terrified, pulsing with adrenaline and fear and horror. My body felt electrified, and parts were throbbing with pain, as if I were a motley blend of the healthy and dying. I couldn't understand anything of the last hour. The only feeling welling up within me was a survival instinct screaming, *Leave!* I knew I couldn't go to my apartment in Galveston; it was too close to Fox. If I could have hopped into an airplane right then, I would have. I drove the car straight for the highway, and I didn't stop driving until I arrived in San Antonio.

I pulled into my dad's driveway around four a.m.

When I got out of the car, the thud of the door closing sounded to me like a bomb went off, but the cool night and the silence of the neighborhood all around remained undisturbed. It felt like the entire world was at peace, and I, a disembodied specter, was the only thing in creation crying out in confusion. I'd driven three and a half hours straight, my mind a frenetic, emotional, stupefying train wreck.

As I looked at my dad's front door and the soft gray cast of shadows on the white house—everything looked so domestic and peaceful—I suddenly felt unutterably exhausted. The quiet night seemed to be seeping into my soul. Urgency and desperation dissipated like vapor into a strange serenity. Then I felt a wave of sympathy for my dad that was so acute it almost felt like pity. The poor man. He was sleeping—communing with God and the angels—who was I to disturb that? *He is at peace.* Compassion for him flooded me, as if he were a child and I wanted to aid his rest. I felt that even if I woke him up, or spoke to him, I wouldn't know how to explain myself anyway—I had no idea how to describe what happened, or what I was even doing there.

So rather than bother him, I opened the rear door of my car, nestled lengthwise in the seat with my backpack for a very uncomfortable and inadequate pillow, and slept.

⌁

I heard a *thump-thump*, a soft rapping sound that seemed to be coming from far away. My consciousness went from black to dark grey, and then to the warm orange sunshine through my eyelids. *Where am I?* I opened my eyes—*oh, the backseat, I remember that*—lifted my head, and—oh, my God, my neck hurt. Snapshots of the incident with Fox flashed through my mind in a jumble of horror and fear. *Really?! That actually happened?* In that moment, I'd rather have woken up in a different life. Turning my head, I looked up. My dad was knocking on the window, grinning from ear to ear.

"Tiff!" He laughed as I opened the door and stiffly stumbled out. "What are you doing sleeping in the driveway? Why didn't you come inside?"

I winced and stood slowly. All of my injuries were concealed under my clothes, but my movements were stiff. His expression quickly changed. He could tell right away that something was not right.

"What happened?" he asked in alarm.

I told him everything—as much as I could remember—but I couldn't look at him and think at the same time. As a result, I was aware only of the height of his body, and its proximity—especially his dock shoes, anchored there in the dewy grass.

"And then," I said, "I finally got out of his apartment and drove here as soon as I left. I'm so sorry, Dad! I didn't know what to do! I didn't want to wake you up, and . . . I don't know. So I just parked and slept in the car. I just didn't know what to do!"

I winced as I turned my head to look at him. Never in my life had I seen my dad's face look quite the way it did at that moment. Not a single muscle moved. Then, when he inhaled and spoke, I realized why.

He was lethally enraged.

He spoke in a measured voice, pronouncing each word in a staccato way, full of ice-cold anger: "Come inside. Walk slowly. I am going to call the police."

THE LONG DARK HOURS OF THE NIGHT—II

He did.

I put my backpack slowly to one side of the chest of drawers in my room and then sat in a small huddled mass, my elbows on my knees, at the foot of my bed. Listening to his voice through the walls as he talked on the phone, I was frozen in embarrassment. *This is too small a thing for the police; this is awful! They're going to laugh about it. Oh, my God! Somehow everybody at school is going to know about this.* I had no idea what to do, but I certainly didn't want the whole school abuzz about it. And somehow, in a weird way, I felt as if it were my fault, like I must have done something wrong or messed up to make Fox act that way. I even wondered why I had driven immediately to San Antonio. It just seemed like the safest place to go.

But I felt like my dad was blowing it out of proportion. I never would have guessed that any official agency, law enforcement or otherwise, would have helped me with something like this. The whole thing, from the violence itself to the unexpected nature of it, just seemed so weird and out of place. I kept thinking, *There must be a reason.* But it turned out that this type of thing was something that the police actually handled. It was called domestic violence, and was an actual crime.

Up until that day, I had never, to my knowledge, even heard the phrase "domestic violence." I don't know if I just missed something in some classes, or lived under a rock while communities everywhere did awareness campaigns. But I did not know the prevalence, features, or dynamics of abuse in the home, or that I could find help.

Fox tried to call me later that morning and left a message. He acted as if no violence whatsoever had happened, but then inexplicably said, "Sorry." He called again hours later and left another voicemail. There was more urgency in his tone; the message was almost frantic. He was wondering where I was. Apparently, he was now conscious of potential ramifications of whatever "hadn't" happened. Maybe he was sobering up. My dad told me to save the messages, and that I did the right thing by coming home to San Antonio.

He came into my room later that afternoon.

"There's a detective on the line. The police need you to tell them what happened, and they'll handle everything from there."

"Okay."

"She's very nice. Just tell her everything you can." He handed me the phone and left the room.

"Hello?" I asked tentatively.

The detective asked detailed questions, and I answered as best I could; I admitted, "I didn't know that this was a big deal. I mean, I thought the police would think it was silly if I called about something like this."

"No one has the right to treat you that way. No one should treat you that way. And if they do, you have protection. You need to know that. Think of it this way: If a stranger did the same thing that your husband did to you, would it be a crime?"

"Well, yes."

"Then that's all you need to know. Just because you know someone pretty well, or have been dating them, or are even related to them, does not give them the right to treat you badly or to be violent. It's abusive. And it's illegal."

"Okay."

"So don't feel ashamed or embarrassed to call the police. You and your dad did exactly the right thing. You did nothing wrong, and it's not your fault."

Geez, is this woman in my head? "Okay . . ."

"I mean that. It's not your fault."

I half chuckled at the repetition. "Okay."

The detective laughed. "Things don't sink in until you hear or see them three times! So what am I going to say next?"

"That it's not my fault."

"That's right. It's not your fault. Now, I'm going to process this stuff and we're going to arrest this guy. Before I go, I want to let you know that you might have a lot of different emotions in the coming days and weeks. Just know that that's normal. You did the right thing by getting out of it. Healing isn't a straight line up. It's more like a curve that goes up and down. Don't get too down in the downs. The ups will come, and you will get through this. Call me if you need anything—anything at all."

"Thank you, Detective."

I hung up. She was so nice, but I felt like a catastrophic mess. Humiliated—by the soft tones she adopted with me, by the fact that to the police I was a victim—I had no intention of ever, ever calling her.

Michael followed through with the police-related issues. Tests loomed in my current classes, but I remained in the refuge of San Antonio. It was nice to be in familiar, safe surroundings. Michael had moved in with his new girlfriend, Beth, a few miles away, though they both stayed at or stopped by Allensworth on occasion, which was how he'd found me in the driveway. While he and Beth worked during the day at their separate jobs and stayed at Magnolia, they came by to check on me as I decompressed at Allensworth. I rested for a couple of days and felt like a huge nuisance inconveniencing my father and Beth. I questioned everything about my life up until that point. Michael had left my room relatively untouched—as if he were saving it for me—and I appreciated it. The little string of green shamrock lights hung in the windows, the Blessed Virgin was in her alcove, and my letterman jacket gathered dust in the closet.

Over those days, he and Beth offered encouragement and support, and gave me some space to think and heal. My dad surprised me with little treats from the H-E-B Central Market nearby—protein shakes, loaves of freshly baked French bread, and the tiny brown dates I used to enjoy while studying Latin. That he remembered all of my favorites, and so specifically, surprised me. I didn't know Beth that well—though it was clear that they cared about each other—and Beth was sincere when she expressed concern about me.

Fox had, when he threw me down so violently, twisted my neck horribly. After I woke up that morning in the driveway, I couldn't move my neck enough to look over my shoulder. The muscles there had all the malleability of rocks and were tender to the touch. Thus, I couldn't drive. When I had more range of motion, a couple days after the attack, Michael drove me back to Galveston. I had just rented and moved into a small house on 18th Street a week or so before the incident; Fox and I were supposed to have lived in it together. It was a cute little place—nothing ostentatious—with large rooms and hardwood floors. One of the reasons that I liked it was that it reminded me of Allensworth.

Fox had finished moving his stuff into the house while I was in San Antonio. (Since he canceled the lease at his apartment to move in with me, he had nowhere else to go.) The day I arrived, the police escorted me to our block and had me sit in a car while they knocked on the front door. My dad followed them. I could hardly believe that Michael would get so close to Fox, who, to me, seemed so fearsome and powerful. But at that moment, I saw in my dad the ferocious intensity of younger days, the hard charger who would rush into a fight, the merest suggestion of the ice-cold road rage at Mardi Gras. I realized I didn't know him at all; I couldn't predict his reactions or his behavior.

I sat in the backseat of the car, terrified. Ever since the incident, I'd had an overwhelming fear of Fox. Obviously, it was understandable that I would be afraid to a certain extent. But the fear I experienced was debilitating: compulsive and withering. In my head, he was capable of incredible, vicious evil—and nobody could stop him. I later learned that victims of domestic violence often display symptoms and thought patterns similar to those of prisoners of war.

The scenario, however, that I feared in my gut that afternoon—sudden violence in which Fox killed all of the police officers and my father, and then sprouted alien devil wings to come after me—did not take place. He answered the door and came out onto the porch. Then, after a short exchange that I couldn't hear, but did see, Fox waited for the handcuffs and got in the waiting cruiser. As body language was all that I had to go on, I watched it closely. What I saw surprised me—*Fox* was the one who was afraid. And of my father! He gave my dad the slightest, almost furtive glance, then kept his distance and didn't make eye contact, instead staying close to the nearest police officer. Compliant and meek, as if he were used to being arrested, he no longer seemed like a warrior-king. He looked like a white-trash alcoholic. My thoughts at the moment took a superficial bent and bordered on amusing: *The police must think I was nuts to hook up with him; what was I thinking? Did he always look like that?*

My dad stayed with me for a few more days and helped take care of more of the police and court-related necessities. An incredibly helpful Galveston sheriff's deputy oversaw a visit from some of Fox's friends to unceremoniously move his stuff back out. Family and friends called every day; my uncle Weston, Michael's brother, who lived close by, also offered to come stay for a while. I had never felt more grateful for the support of family in my life, but after the incident I started to become a tiny wisp of my former self.

I was stuck in that night. I had not thought I would live through it. The blast of unexpected violence—shocking, horrific—was more than I could understand. I remembered the look on Fox's face, the absence of consciousness in his eyes, as if he had been taken over by a demon, and even now I could feel the hate and mindless brutality in his hands. The cruel things he had done just to be cruel.

I thought he loved me. I never thought he would do that.
I should have known.

I had finally let go and trusted somebody. I decided to align with someone else and establish myself—to trust in life and thus God—for once, after all of these years of being cautious. I'd decided that, rather than being strong and alone, I would unite. And look where it got me.

THE LONG DARK HOURS OF THE NIGHT—III

I felt as if I were dying inside. I couldn't trust anyone or anything—not even myself or my own judgment. I had tried to create something wonderful, almost a dream come true, in the form of a steady, happy union. It had been such a risk for me, even down to the simple act of Fox moving into my new house. I had heard that when car bombs go off in places like Israel or Pakistan, the thing that the first responders notice is the leaves: that there are no leaves on the trees. I felt like I was watching, in shock, the leaves fall from a vast explosion. My soul and mind collapsed upon themselves, rapidly retreating until I was watching my own life unfold, without care or regard, from the shores of a dark and lonely land.

My dad seemed to sense it. Those few days that he was in Galveston with me, he turned his body more often fully toward mine and—perhaps unconsciously—leaned his head just a tiny bit forward and down, as if he were coaxing a small child or a pet to come out from a hiding place. He made intentional eye contact and, through it, appeared to try to order me more alive. He patted me gently on the back and the shoulders more often, affectionate and encouraging. I normally appreciated small gestures—I used to love it when my dad ruffled my hair. But if something was really wrong, hugs and physical closeness made me feel claustrophobic. I tended to calm down faster if I had some space, and at that time, human touch felt empty and unwanted, like a Band-Aid for a gash it couldn't possibly cover.

Michael tried to help in every way imaginable. He took me to the nicest grocery store on Galveston Island. There he proceeded to buy more groceries than I had ever seen in one cart in my life—five to ten each of whatever he knew my favorites to be, and single items that he thought I might need. I followed behind him like a quiet, sad shadow. He lavished me with supplies, and I realized, even at the time and through the void, that he was trying to sustain me. I saw it; I thought I understood it. But I could not respond. Where I normally drew energy, there was just a space.

Back at the house, he paced purposefully all over the retro black-and-white-checkered floor of my kitchen, putting away the bits and pieces of his affection in my kitchen cabinets. After he had put the provisions away, he got ready to leave. He had done everything he could, but he could not be away from San Antonio and work anymore. He apologized, but there was nothing he needed to be sorry for.

By his stance, I knew that he was just awaiting inspiration, a signal, permission to do anything else that he could to help. But it never came. There was nothing else to do. No one could wade through the black waters of life for me. If I was to live and be happy, I needed to find a source of strength and meaning for myself—by myself.

He looked sad. He lingered in the kitchen. He lingered in the small living room, standing in his upright way on the beautiful hardwood floor. A soft breeze came from the small fan and when my dad opened the front door to let himself out, we both felt the wave of heat from the sun-baked porch.

I thanked him. I tried to rally, to reassure him that I would be okay. But I did not believe it myself, and we both knew it. I said good-bye, half expecting to never see him again. Between the darkness I felt within and what Fox might do when he got out of jail, I didn't think I would live that long. He said good-bye too, but in a different way. His eyes were alert and his voice firm; totally present in the moment, he believed in the future.

I did not feel anything spectacular at that moment, but I became strangely aware of *something*. I could not have said what it was. It was like comfort, or unity; however, the bright reality was only the merest speck in my mind, like a far-off star. But for days and months and years afterward, even to this very day, I have remembered it. Michael said good-bye and hugged me. With one last concerned look and a wave, he drove away.

I threw myself into school with what little energy I had. I figured out how to make the Galveston days pass, minimizing the pain as much as possible, sometimes losing myself in the sunny beaches in the afternoon and books in the evening. I avoided contact with my friends at school; I didn't want to bring them down. Sometimes recovery just involved a lot of trying to breathe and not self-destruct as the warm, dark evenings passed, minute after minute. I found myself washing dishes one night—a set of expensive, sharp knives—and wondering how quickly I would die if I stabbed myself in the chest right then. Sometimes I just sat alone in a dark room, feeling crazed, crying, unable to function or face the world. It took everything I had, especially during the first few months, to study and attend classes. I didn't like the idea of medication or taking drugs to get by somehow—I wanted to find or make the strength within myself to get through.

My birthday came and went. Two birthday cards arrived, one from each of my parents. I cherished them: Up they went on the mantel in the living room, where they stayed for the rest of the school year. The cards were the only things in the room, and I preferred that room to all the others. In the evenings, the sun shone through the windows and turned the entire space into a bowl of light. Every part of the bare room lit up as though it were encrusted in gold. I liked it empty. There was very little furniture in the house. I'd never had much to begin with, having used the furniture in the dorms, and I felt money was better spent on food and weekend trips back to San Antonio than a sofa or a dining room table.

Exercise became a great relief. I worked out at home, not wanting to face the people in a gym. The effort of working out, the exertion, forced me to focus my mind, and my body just happened, as a fringe benefit, to get stronger. I tried to annihilate myself in the workout sessions. I hated myself. I hated my inner weakness—feeling so sad and so scared of Fox and adrift in life in general.

During one particularly difficult night, I was prone on the floor in my bedroom after a complicated sequence of strength training, and all of a sudden I felt a touch. It wasn't a physical touch. It felt like a strong sunbeam might feel if it had hands and arms—except that it was approaching eleven o'clock at night and there was no sun. The touch landed on my upper back and extended throughout my body. A gentle, pervasive feeling of peace radiated through me, almost against my will and certainly outside of my effort. It was unlike anything I had ever experienced, and the first feeling of relief and peace that I had had in weeks. For a long moment, I rested in the light and the comfort. Eyes closed against the world, and brimming with gratitude, I muttered against the fibers of the carpet, "Thank you, God."

There was a crisis center in Galveston that helped with sexual assault and domestic violence cases. The Galveston police, in conjunction with that center, pursued a protective order against Fox on my behalf. The judge found that abuse and violence had occurred; the order was signed, official. With the protective order in place, Fox wasn't to contact me or come within a certain distance of me, my home, or my work for two years. And I could get into as much trouble as he could. As crazy as it might sound, some days I wanted Fox back desperately. Sometimes that protective order was the only thing that kept me from knocking on his door to tell him how much I loved him. That crisis center, over the course of the year after the incident, got the protective order, finalized the divorce, everything. Apparently the marriage couldn't be annulled, but I didn't care. I was so grateful for the legal assistance that the fact the marriage was on the books just seemed to me like divine retribution for a bad decision: Yep, I made a mistake.

The Galveston police detective had told me that the healing process wouldn't be a straight line. And it wasn't. Every day was a roller coaster with modest ups (barely perceptible) and deep, deep downs. During one of the downs, my whole being was consumed by a living, breathing, desperate darkness. I was sick and I needed help: I knew that. But I didn't think any human being could offer the aid or answers I needed. If I told anyone what I really believed—that life was a hellacious, disappointing battlefield of broken dreams and pain—they would think I was crazy. They wouldn't understand. I wasn't crazy; I just hurt. Everything in life hurt.

I will either do this by myself or I will die.

My mom called me almost every day after the incident with Fox, trying to encourage and support me. A couple months into those evening discussions, she confided that my father had been violent with her when she was pregnant with Mark: He had tried to strangle her in the living room, and it was that event that prompted her to get divorced.

I didn't doubt her for a moment: I remembered Michael's reckless rage on the Louisiana highway; how he had been consumed by anger. Beset by horror and revulsion, as if he were some kind of monster and I hadn't realized it, I thought of his fury suddenly as a beast within that lurked—that he didn't know enough about, or care enough to control—and it surfaced in horrible, unexpected ways. My mom added, "You saw it. You were standing in the doorway."

I flashed immediately back to the nightmares I had as a child. The doorway and the terror. The feeling that I had never known strength. The dreams that caused me to curl up in a terrified ball, wondering why I was so messed up: the only daughter in the world who didn't trust or like her dad. The only one who was afraid.

They were memories.

For weeks after that call with my mom, I wasn't quite sure what to think. I continued talking with Michael on the phone every week or so as if nothing had happened; I pretended everything was normal. I had never trusted him completely, but he had been so protective and helpful recently. Even though things had been more distant between us since I started college, I couldn't just toss him away mentally into a "used to be" pile. The right thing to do, I knew in my heart of hearts, would be to love—not "love" in the sense of the plain old happy feeling, but "love," the excruciating expansion of the heart that manifests itself in action, through pain, to show support and forgiveness. But I didn't believe I had the strength.

I felt so much anger.

I could fake affection for him, but then I was just an actor. I wanted to be fully real, to know my own heart and speak it out into the world. I despised the fact that he didn't stand and face me when it came to big things, like the incident with my mom. Why hadn't he ever told me about that? Even if he felt ashamed, knew it was wrong, had changed—I wanted to know his side of the story. I felt like he'd never told the truth: How he really felt, what he wanted, who he was.

All I wanted was the truth.

Courage welled up—I wanted to confront him—but an old cowardice was right on its heels, loud and strong. I feared that, if I confronted him about the incident with my mom and everything else, his assistance would evaporate. I didn't think whatever love he had for me could withstand my barrage of anger. I thought I needed his support to live; I couldn't make it on my own. So I decided, in a flaming heap of hypocrisy and self-disgust, to stay quiet.

My weight plummeted. During a trip to see my mom, she had commented, genuinely concerned, that I looked "skeletal." I didn't care. Some people turn to food when they're under pressure; I turned away from it. But gradually, I got back on my feet—emotionally and financially. I still staggered and swayed, but I moved forward.

Every now and then I felt intense anger at Fox. He had spent his life breaking mental barriers in order to take military action—but now where was he? I had thought of him as a warrior, a genuinely good man who used his strength, both inner and outer, for the good of others. But I'd immersed myself in a fantasy storyline—idealizing him as a Hollywood-version of a SEAL: disciplined, manly, and brave. I saw clearly now his lack of respect, and it crushed me. I felt violated. Fox had unusual willpower and courage, but it was buried under a heap of stereotypical ideas about women, a destructive reliance on physical strength to resolve conflict, and a life he had built around alcohol and, to a certain extent, vanity. "SEAL" was a brand name, not necessarily the mark of a person who possessed the courage and dignity to uplift—support and encourage—those around him. Fox simply couldn't handle other people and his own mind.

And I had played into it—hook, line, and sinker.

How?

I despaired of finding the man I wanted. I questioned everything. What were reliance and respect? What was a good relationship? Once you had expanded the mind to the outer reaches of violence and threat, how could you return to love and caring for people? Would you even want to? Would you even recognize love—or believe it—if you saw it? Wouldn't you always live with one foot in the deep end of hell, even at home?

I sat in my room sometimes, my head in my hands, just trying to wrap my brain around the meaning of it all. How was I going to learn from this, make it something good? Sometimes my frustration with Fox was redirected, peculiarly, at my dad as well. With Fox, I felt deeply unwanted—almost despised—and unprotected. I didn't realize it at the time, but it all related to my dad. The sense of isolation, of me having to fight and survive alone. I had no idea how much I had missed Michael's presence in my life. My mother had—through no fault of her own—been a fierce, all-consuming force that almost swallowed my identity: There was no balance. Now I was struggling to figure out men and masculinity by myself.

Michael, at this time, was in the background; I didn't reach out to him. His aid now felt more contrived. In a way, he was one of "them"—one of them who might hurt me. As we were mostly apart again, my heart reverted back to the way I felt growing up: as if he weren't really around.

I had, quite simply, no idea what constituted a good man.

In my wanderings throughout Galveston early on in college, I had discovered a small café downtown called Mod. A trendy, comfortable coffeehouse, Mod had plenty of space to study, a secluded upper level, and colorful café tables with handmade collages on the tabletops. I enjoyed it and went quite often to study or just enjoy a cup of coffee. Since the incident, Mod and its quiet ambience had become a refuge for me. Fox was more likely to be found at a bar, so I didn't worry so much that he would intrude—either by design or by accident. One day, I went into the café, and an employee, a young man named Wyatt, asked out of the blue, "Hey, do you want to work here?"

I looked around the café like I was suddenly seeing it for the first time. I replied, delighted, "Sure!"

So I started working at Mod.

I loved it. As depressed as I was in private, compounded by the pressure and responsibilities of college, Mod gave me a sense of purpose and routine. My coworkers, as well as the owners—Joe and Denise—were kind, uplifting, and considerate people. Two coworkers in particular—Aaron, a tall guy with a silly streak, and Fred, a dark-haired young man—became my buddies. They, I think, sensed that I suffered a bit, but to their credit they didn't ever say anything; they seemed to appreciate my company as much as I enjoyed theirs. When Fred found out I liked the Magnetic Fields' "69 Love Songs," he made sure the CD was in the café's multidisk music system. Often, when I arrived for work, its tracks played softly in the background.

One day, as I was leaving my afternoon shift at Mod, having cleaned up the tables and straightened the umbrellas outside, Aaron took me aside, "Hey, Tiff, do you want me to walk you to your car?"

I looked at him, surprised. Aaron and I were close, but in all the time that I'd worked at Mod, he had never offered to do that. "No, uh, thanks, I think I'll be fine," I said slowly. My car, after all, was just across the street, and I could see it from the coffeehouse. But Aaron seemed mildly alarmed and protective. I added, "Why? Did you see something?"

He looked through the large front window with a slight frown. "I didn't like the look of that guy on the bicycle. He was watching you strangely while you were cleaning up outside."

"Really?" I said, suddenly alarmed. "What guy?" I looked out.

There, on a bicycle across the street, sat Carter, a friend of mine from school I'd hung out with before dating Fox. My surprise instantly turned into relief; I was just grateful "that guy" wasn't Fox. It had been almost two years since the incident, but unceasing fear haunted everything I did, sometimes flashing forth in a wave of real terror.

Carter was a down-to-earth man, authentic and extremely funny. An ex-army soldier—a tanker—he now served in the Texas National Guard as a sergeant and had to go away some weekends for drill. Carter knew who he was and people could take it or leave it, even down to chewing tobacco in the back of the church for his friend's wedding. I admired the unapologetic audacity of being himself and speaking his mind. But that didn't explain the question, *What is he doing here?*

He wouldn't mean any harm, but it was odd that he chose to loiter across the street. I turned to Aaron and grabbed his arm; I felt intense affection for him. "Aaron, thank you for offering; I really appreciate it. But I know that guy, and he's not going to hurt me. He's a classmate of mine from school."

I took off my barista apron and, grabbing my purse, strode out the door into the warm Galveston sunshine. I walked across the street, heading straight for Carter.

"Hey," I said.

"Hey."

"What are you doing here?"

"I saw you putting stuff away and wanted to talk to you."

"What about?"

"Uh, just to see how you're doing," he replied vaguely.

I knew he knew about the incident with Fox. Most of my class-mates did. Texas A&M at Galveston was a small school. A lot of people tended to believe Fox's version of events, because he was charismatic and talked a lot—whereas I stayed silent—and which varied, according to the person, from nothing at all happening that evening to my freaking out in some form or another. But save for a few friends, I had lost the desire to defend myself in others' opinions. People could believe what they wanted to; I knew the truth. As a result of my silence, I fancied a lot of people were against me or thought I was a liar, but I didn't feel up to fighting for my reputation. I was too busy trying to scrape by and survive.

"I'm fine," I answered. *Well, not really. I want to kill myself half the time.*

"Well, uh, I'm sorry about what happened with Fox. He's changed a lot recently. Done some weird stuff and gotten into trouble and, well, I don't trust him anymore."

"Well, that's probably good."

"I miss you."

My heart collapsed in a puddle; I suddenly felt so lonely.

"I miss you too, Carter."

"If you, uh, want to hang out sometime, I'd like to see you again."

"Thanks. Maybe I'll give you a call. You still have the same number?" I hadn't called him in more than a year.

"Yeah."

"All right. Well, take care."

"You, too."

❧

Carter and I started seeing each other as the last semester of senior year rolled around. I felt noncommittal and cautious; nevertheless, we enjoyed each other's company, going out to dinner or for bike rides around town, cooking out on the grill (one of Carter's favorite pastimes), or just studying together. Every month he left for one weekend to go to drill with the Army National Guard, which he called "playing army." He complained, saying the work used to be fun when he was with the guys, but now it was all paperwork and bullshit. But I could see his heart was in it: He loved the army.

At school, it was soon time, for those who wanted one, to order the Texas A&M college ring. The "Aggie ring" was a big deal. Stories were passed around of how Texas Aggies got jobs, and even spouses, just wearing their rings around the right people at the right time. I didn't really see the need to spend the money, but asked my dad about it one day anyway. He exclaimed, "Oh, geez, Tiff! Get the ring!"

His response surprised me. He seemed flabbergasted that I would consider not getting it. To him, mementos of camaraderie and significance like the Aggie ring were treasures in life. I was, by now, mostly solvent and independent, so I saved up and ordered it. When it arrived, I picked it up at the student body office in the center of the small campus. The first glints of gold twinkled and I grinned. I put it on as I walked through the same lobby I'd entered as a brand-new student four years earlier. The metal felt cold and hard against my hand. So very real. I suddenly wondered whether maybe something meaningful would happen now to me, when I was wearing my ring.

As the academic year came to a close, I still didn't know what I wanted to do for work after college. Not only that, but Carter found out that his Army National Guard unit would be deploying to Iraq within the next year. I fretted about his safety—and worried about my own. Depression hovered nearby, like an uninvited dinner guest who was quite familiar. I was afraid of engaging in the everyday. I feared what life held in store.

My dad had married Beth on Independence Day near the Alamo in San Antonio several months before. Neither Mark nor I was able to make it for the wedding ceremony, but I was happy for him. Things felt a little more distant between us now, but he seemed happy. I liked Beth, and Michael had been alone so long that I was glad he finally found someone. My mom and Mark lived two thousand miles away in the San Francisco Bay Area, where she worked and Mark studied; Guy was still in Modesto.

While talking with my mom one night, she suggested that I move to California after graduation and spend some time at a meditation center in Oakland. It was called an ashram and had a limited selection of rooms that visitors and residents, all devotees of the meditation lineage, could live in for free or, in some cases, at a minimal cost. She worked in the volunteer department at the ashram and loved it. There were chants and prayers in the morning, meditations throughout the day, and sometimes events in the evening—everything was focused on looking within to experience God. She encouraged me to come to the ashram to heal, to spend some time relaxing until I decided what I wanted to do. As I practiced yoga and meditated at home in Galveston often, I could see that there might be a real benefit to the idea. I agreed to go; I simply didn't know what else to do.

Well, I thought at the time, *I suppose weeks of praying can't hurt.*

꩜

I graduated from Texas A&M University at Galveston in May. I saw Carter a couple days before, to say good-bye; I didn't know whether we'd meet again. I kept looking away from him and those trusting blue eyes. The prospect of Iraq loomed like a black cloud; I didn't want him to die or get wounded or captured. I tried to avoid thinking about the possibility. I assured him I would send him care packages while he was overseas if he'd send me his address once he knew it.

The graduation ceremony was simple. My mom, Guy, and Mark flew in from California; my dad and Beth drove in from San Antonio. After all the years, the ceremony seemed anticlimactic. I'd learned far more from my mistakes in life than I ever did from writing reports on ships and inland waterways. The diploma was just something for the world to see. Proof of some achievement, maybe a whispered hint of future success.

I felt it to be so very, very far from the truth.

THE LETTER

Immediately following graduation, I drove to California and moved into the Oakland ashram. It was a quiet, reflective kind of place, full of the pleasant smells of frankincense and fresh flowers—very different from the Galveston area, with its mildewing wharves and sea breezes carrying the scent of rotting seaweed. The ashram felt safe, pristine, and holy. I had prayed before, but I normally approached praying as if God were a bit like a doctor: I spelled out pressing issues and asked for them to get fixed somehow. A couple of thoughts, a few scattered thanks, and then I was finished. My prayers were genuine, but I didn't normally put all of my being into freely communing with God. I was, to tell the truth, a little pissed off at God.

But at the ashram, meditation and prayer became transformative for me. The first few days I had no idea what was going on. My primary goal was to not look ridiculous or do something stupid. I tried to blend in, muttering quietly during the Sanskrit chants so nobody realized I didn't know what the words were. When it was time for meditation, I sat quietly, closed my eyes, and attempted to make it through until the bell gonged and the meditation period was over. Sometimes I felt like a sprinter, starved of oxygen, just trying to make it to the finish line. I aimed to not move or make noise, so as not to disturb the silent and holy people around me who obviously knew what they were doing, and I tried not to scream aloud in frustration that the meditations were too damn long. The meditation room was dark, quiet, and still. And I was about to lose my mind.

There is a place in that ashram called the hall. It is an enormous room made for the larger gatherings, full of prayer books and warm red blankets for the participants. (The hall can get quite cold, and the meditators use the blankets to wrap around their shoulders for warmth.) Early on in my stay, I would open the heavy door into the hall and sit down to meditate when the large room was completely empty. The hall, then, felt full of God. But God didn't seem particularly inclined to cater to me. Everything felt vast and powerful, and I seemed meaningless and ignorant. Insecure and uncomfortable, I worried that my presence somehow polluted the unsullied nature of the place.

I wanted to get better at meditation, this practice of concentration, or praying, or focus, whatever it was. So I deliberately spent time alone in the hall, trying to hammer my way into awareness of God. It sucked. I felt, in alternating and sometimes simultaneous waves, pressing floods of grief, or shame, or frustration—all of which seemed like they might swallow me whole. It took all of my discipline to just sit there, physically still, while my soul and heart got dragged behind the crazed mustang of my mind.

However, as those solitary trips accumulated, I actually began to sense some progress. At first my thoughts were riotous, so emotionally charged that I sometimes felt physical pain in the act of staying still. But soon, I started to feel more tranquil. Then sometimes there was a faint sense of arising—and I realized it was my own heart rising up into my awareness, a living and real force, finally feeling safe enough and free enough to come forward out of the hole into which I'd beaten it daily.

I began to understand that meditation was like the deepest kind of conversation, a communion with one's own heart and its truth—and through it, the presence and grace of God. I started to sit still for longer, and get deeper into different kinds of peace, to understand (sometimes) when my mind was my own worst enemy. Praying became an active endeavor—something that could actually change my own understanding of myself and the world around me. In my better moments, I looked for God as for a friend, and found that, when at my best and happiest, I sought for God as for the love of my life.

Now, all of that sounds remarkably neat and orderly. It was not. I cried every night I was there, desperately wanting Fox (even then, more than two years later), worrying about Carter, stressing about what I was going to do for work. To be clear, the process wasn't a pleasant linear progression of insight; it was more like mucking about in a swamp and then suddenly seeing new things.

But I was determined.

Michael was not in the picture much. In fact, after I graduated I don't even remember talking to him for several months. Our relationship had broken down dramatically. We had separate concerns now: him, his married life, and me, the efforts to start a meaningful life of my own. Ever since we were relatively close during high school, the slow shift apart—first in Galveston, then afterward—seemed especially broad and harsh. At least in college, I'd been able to focus on classes and the future. But now I had no promising lights on the horizon. I noticed his absence keenly.

His silence let my mind create its own reality. I began to believe he didn't actually want to help or be in my life. I was more like a burden and an inconvenience to him. The distance and awkwardness didn't surprise me. I always half expected him to fade out of my life again. But it would have been nice to have more kindness between us, to have someone to adore. My lack of success now wasn't helping my sense of confidence; I began to think it validated that I was a useless, oxygen-guzzling leech in the world.

Occasionally, soft feelings arose and said I should make an effort to keep in touch with him. Later, sometimes Michael himself even made an overture. But for now I had an involuntarily brittle distance within me.

I defaulted to life as I knew it best: Life without him.

❦

My training and background, such as they were, were not in areas I wanted to pursue. I'd finished the maritime administration program simply because I didn't want to delay getting my bachelor's degree by transferring to another major. I fumbled, increasingly lost, looking for purpose and meaningful work. But the months passed with little forward progress. Spinning around in ineffectual circles, I frustrated myself and my family. I went on a short road trip to Mexico with Guy; I lived briefly with my wonderful friend Lorraine from college and tried to find work in New Orleans; I tried living in different cities in California.

Throughout my wanderings, I sent Carter care packages with home-baked goodies. At first, he shared them with his buddies, but one time they ate so many that he had started to hide and hoard the best treats for himself. He especially liked a little pastry called "Orange Chocolate Triangles" and asked for more, but he also requested that I not sprinkle as much confetti into the box, saying, "Tiff, it's nice and I really appreciate the thought, but this last time was overkill. I opened it and was like, 'Dang!' It went everywhere; I think there are still pink-flamingo confetti bits in the camper on base."

I actually had my feelings a little hurt by that. When Michael was overseas with the army in Bosnia, he seemed to enjoy little surprises; I thought Carter would too. I'd looked all over for Florida-themed confetti because he liked Kenny Chesney's music. He said it kept him sane over there in Iraq (debatable)—and he'd always wanted to go to the Florida Keys. It took me a while to find those pink flamingos. But what could I complain about? He was the one working convoy escort duty, watching for improvised bombs on overpasses, and going through the most dangerous cities in the Middle East.

Beyond trying to help Carter feel better overseas, giving him a friend and anchor in life, and trying to understand myself better while looking for meaningful work, I felt incredibly frustrated: socially and professionally impotent. Goodwill was in the red. In the last year and a half, I'd done nothing of lasting significance or made, as I perceived it, a positive contribution to anything of real consequence. I questioned whether I'd ever get traction in life. I was living in California—in Modesto again, of all places—and had a job as an assistant to the owner of a small company. My mom tried to help me; she listened to and encouraged me, and even surprised me with gifts like clothes for work. She had no means of helping more, but at least we talked every day. My dad, on the other hand, was nowhere to be found. I didn't call him often; nor did he call me, and when we did talk, it was a frigid, surface kind of conversation—as if we were skating on thin ice above a deep and dense sea.

One day, I found an old pendant in a worn treasure box full of trinkets. It was my tarnished part of the "Best Friends" necklace from so many years ago—the one I had shared with him at Castle Air Force Base. I felt disappointment and pain as I looked at it. My feelings for him were just a chasm, a wasteland. Suddenly, raw, red-hot anger coursed through me.

I was a fool. As if he ever cared, or even kept his half.

I threw it away. I felt no regret. I wanted to be free of any reminders of him and the past forever. The strand sounded metallically against itself, and the trash bag made a crinkling noise as the pendant slid down. My fury grew. I couldn't stay quiet any longer. I sat down and wrote him a long letter, full of details and the past. I didn't skimp. I never planned to talk to him again; for once and for all, I was going to be completely honest, come hell or high water. I loved honesty; I wasn't always honest myself—with others, sometimes I just didn't want to start a fight; and with myself, I often didn't want to admit that I hurt—but I knew it felt good and pure. I wanted, for once, to achieve it.

Sentences became explosives to completely destroy every bridge that spanned between us. I felt as if he supplied me with an image of a parent rather than the substantive, living force of a father. I addressed all the time he was gone while Mark and I were growing up; the sense in me that he was untrustworthy; the fact that he had attacked my mom while I watched, and that on some level I'd remembered it. I told him how it had always bothered me, but I didn't understand how or why—and how much I hated him for it. Not just the fact he did it, but the fact that he never came clean about it. I wished he'd approached me and said he'd made a terrible mistake; that he had described what he'd learned from it about himself, about others, and about love. That he had found a way to integrate and overcome: That he was now a better person. That was, in my opinion, where the real power in parenting was. Not in being perfect! But in sharing who he was—and how he approached the difficulties of life. It was the angriest letter I had ever written in my life. My intention was for it to be the truth—and for nothing to be left in its wake. I didn't plan on talking to him again. In a way, it was my means of starting afresh.

I *should* have written it—I needed to, in order to get it out. But after writing it, I could have waited a day. Reread it. Rereading it might have been horrifying enough to convince me not to send the thing. As I look back now, I realize that all I wanted was for him to *talk with me*—to tell me how he felt about life, what he had done (even if it was wrong), why he did it, and how he felt about it now. Even though I wanted truthfulness myself, I wasn't actually demonstrating, by example, what I wanted. Honesty would have been: *Dad, I hurt a lot and I feel like you're not around. Why aren't you around? Don't you love me? Am I not a good person?* But I didn't see that hurt in me at the time; all I saw was anger.

And so . . . I sent it.

As soon as I couldn't take it back, I was body-slammed by sender's remorse. Distress hit every nook and cranny of my psyche, smearing me with self-loathing and regret. Second-guessing my decision, I felt my normal sensitivity and care surge forward. I'd given in to weakness. I should have stayed quiet; I didn't want to hurt him. But another part of me said that he had to know. He wasn't facing up and playing straight with me. He wasn't doing *anything*. A part of me was fed up. I wanted openness and truthfulness from him more than anything else, and was willing to watch everything else fall if I couldn't have it.

I waited, tense and angry, in case he responded.

He never did.

ST. JOSEPH

L ater that week, I completely regretted sending the letter. I mentally reviewed passages of it in my head and cringed at the hate and the lack of gratitude in them. I thought I was being fair—but I wasn't. Anyone who read the letter would think I was the most spoiled and ungrateful person in the world. But they couldn't understand. And even now I didn't know how I could have done it better. And at least it was out there. Somehow, that was a relief. Some days I felt better knowing that I said what I felt as best I could at the time. Even if it made him upset, even if it wasn't the entire truth as I felt it now, at least I'd said it.

﹏

Months later, while visiting some friends in Modesto, I passed St. Joseph's Catholic Church, a large, one-story complex off of Oakdale Road, relatively close to Beyer, my old school, but easy to overlook. Years before, Mark and I used to ride our bikes by the sanctuary on the way to school. One time when Michael was in town, he took us to a Mass at that church. It was the only time that I had been inside the sanctuary.

I should go inside and pray.

I hadn't prayed at all recently. Maybe that would help me feel better. I took a few steps in, and suddenly the Blessed Virgin Mary was staring at me.

Almost stepping out from the massive, beautiful piece of artwork on the wall, Our Lady of Guadalupe, wearing her cloak of stars, seemed to be telling me something. But I couldn't quite grasp the message. I knew one thing, though: I was supposed to be in there. I sat down in a pew in a room nearby, slightly off the main sanctuary. The pew groaned and shifted with my weight. I closed my eyes, grateful for the privacy and the peaceful air, and I prayed.

The first thing I did was apologize.

❧

Very soon thereafter, Carter returned from Iraq and begged me to move to Texas and live with him. I had reservations about the idea. Despite the fact that Carter was quite literally the most truthful man I had ever met, he could also be, to my way of thinking, intensely oppositional on occasion. When we dated in Galveston, we had spats about ridiculous things, like whether or not the TV ought to be on, or what to cook for dinner—every single time we got together. On top of the depression I already fought every day, which made me feel exhausted, our constant arguing drained my energy even more. It took so much effort to just make him understand how I felt.

He was a Midwestern boy raised in dismal poverty; even now, he hated oatmeal because he had had it every day for breakfast growing up. I was a middle-class girl who had, by then, lived in many different places and whose parents (Mom and all three dads) had instilled a distinct spiritual bent into her character. I was often unrealistic and impractical; I didn't recognize the effort and resources it took to have the things I'd just . . . well, grown up with. I don't think I was spoiled, per se, but some people might. I had enough *stuff* growing up, but I never really felt like I had connected with loved ones the way that I wanted to. Carter and I loved each other, but we were, as he put it, "an odd couple." He knew I had a good heart, but sometimes he believed I had my head in the stratosphere.

However, he badgered, pleaded, and nagged me, and eventually I agreed to move to Texas and live with him. I told him outright that I didn't want to get married, that I would be his girlfriend and help him in every way that I could—in my mind this involved helping him transition back to civilian life, because it was very clear to me that Iraq had left some deep marks on Carter—but I wanted to adjust his expectations. I kept repeating it—and he said he understood. He said he did want to get married, but he respected my position. I believe, in retrospect, that he thought he could win me over if he could just get me to Texas.

Unfortunately Carter was asking for something that I could not offer: namely, someone who had her own life together. I now had a deep distrust of anything called "permanent," and a cynical aversion to commitment. As far as I was concerned, I was through trying to live my bigger, heartfelt dreams. Life was a rough and dark place; I could only try to do little things to help people and be a nice person. So I decided to support Carter and trudge, uninspired, through this mess of existence. (My journal entries through this period were so dark, twisted, and dismal I cannot even stand to read them for very long now. I honestly wonder sometimes what Carter even saw in me.)

When I moved to Texas, I didn't trust anyone enough to rely on them in a substantial way. I was acutely, painfully fearful of anything in my life that required another person's help or support. I tried to eliminate and minimize all of the ways that people could disappoint and hurt me. Naturally, that effort on my part didn't lend itself well to dating. I don't think Carter understood how deeply the incident with Fox had affected me.

From the moment I landed in Texas and we drove to "our" new apartment in Galveston, Carter and I alternately squabbled with and supported each other.

I soon interviewed for a community education position that was available at the very same Resource and Crisis Center (RCC) that had assisted me after the incident with Fox. The supervisor, Beverly, surprised me with her strong presence and intelligence. She sat across from me at the table, just getting to know me, and then threw a curveball, asking, "What do you think has been your biggest failure in life?"

Whoa, I thought. *Good for you, lady!* I liked that kind of direct, meaningful questioning.

"I'd have to think about that," I said. I sat quietly for a moment, searching my heart for its saddest place. I thought of embarrassments and minor failures, of Ajax and Fox, but then my mind lit on a strange fact—a boy from Beyer who had committed suicide. He had never been a close friend of mine, but I could have been more caring toward him. Then I thought of both my mom and Michael, and the many sacrifices they had made. *Yes*, my heart said, *that's it*. I replied, "I think . . . my biggest failure in life has been not appreciating the people around me—really appreciating them—while I was with them."

"Hmm," she said, evaluating me with a brighter look in her eyes, "that's a beautiful answer."

A couple days later, I had the job.

And so I worked in the Galveston area, conducting classes and trainings on the nature of domestic violence and sexual assault, talking to everyone from police officers to first graders. I enjoyed the challenge of the job—a lot of times I had to educate *myself* a day or even hours before a presentation. It was exhausting but extremely rewarding: I was finally able to use my skills of adapting to and connecting with people to send an important message. I wanted to protect everyone—to make them wise enough to recognize weakness and violence in others and themselves. I also wanted to inspire those who were either being abused or abusing others to understand that there *was* something higher and happier in life than living in fear or anger.

But after just a summer at that nonprofit community agency, I was worn out. The turnover in community service organizations like the RCC is high, because the pay is often quite low and the work is emotionally draining. Carter got hired at an oil services job in Houston at about the same time I started to feel completely depleted by the breakneck pace and constant flow of the battered, injured, depressed, and forgotten of society. I'd have to find another job when we moved to Houston, but that was okay. I was ready for a change; I felt like I'd learned a lot and done some good, but knew that a life in the nonprofit sector serving victims of domestic violence was not my path. It took a thicker skin than mine to carry through the frenetic, painful days.

~∀~

When Carter and I moved to Houston and finally got settled, I looked for work. All other outlying fronts in life seemed steady, if remote. My mom and Mark were okay in California; I hadn't heard from Michael but assumed he was just living his life and doing fine. I had reconciled myself to the fact that, essentially, my father and I were estranged and, barring some unlikely cataclysmic shift in communication, would remain so. I didn't worry much about it; my pressing priority was right in front of me. The job market in Houston was far larger and had more corresponding opportunities, but the search was nevertheless frustrating. Beverly at the RCC had written me a glowing letter of recommendation, but it didn't help if I couldn't even secure an interview. However, after months of fruitless leads, I managed to get the job I wanted.

I started working at Post Oak, a marketing firm in Houston. I served as a resourceful assistant to the president of the company, Eric. Balancing various client meetings and marketing projects suited me perfectly. I enjoyed work. I finally felt appreciated and needed, and that satisfaction gave me internal momentum, the energy and enthusiasm to pursue new projects. The company worked closely with the Catholic Archdiocese of Galveston-Houston and handled a lot of projects relating to promoting Catholic schools in the region.

In the course of my workdays, I collaborated with a lot of people in Houston. I loved meeting with different clients. I did not, however, love driving around Houston. It was a tense and materialistic city compared to San Antonio, and I found the pretentious shopping malls, endless intersections with long lines of cars, and the traffic around the Galleria area to be annoying. Beyond the fact that I didn't much care for much of the city of Houston itself, work was great. One collaborator I often worked with, Anna, was a young woman who coordinated projects at the archdiocesan development office. I could tell she was very smart and had an excellent sense of humor, but we only ever talked on the phone or exchanged e-mails. One day, during a client visit with Eric, I finally met her.

Anna greeted me with plain business courtesy, but her dark eyes sparkled with wit. We exchanged routine pleasantries, professional and cautious. A few months later, I met her for lunch at La Madeleine near Rice University to discuss some project-related issues. We laughed together into the afternoon. Talking shop revealed synergy; each of us found an unexpected friend. Anna was a dynamo, working tirelessly throughout the day from her office in downtown Houston and sometimes lighting up my e-mail with scathing witticisms. We often grabbed drinks together in the evenings after work, to chat about political, social, and personal absurdities. Anna started to tease me: "Tiffany, get out of my head! I've warned you before: *The dark bunnies will get you!*"

Every day at Post Oak was different, and I continued working with my colleagues, including Anna, happy to be part of an efficient team and doing our best to further the firm's projects. I tried to be patient when things went awry, and was quick to fix things when possible. Inspired by some of the work that the Catholic schools did to promote themselves (including official seals and mascots), I decided to approach Incarnate Word High School in San Antonio about the possibility of creating a professional, unique "shamrock" design. The administration was interested, but money was tight. I tried to nurture the project along, amid all of the other efforts at Post Oak, but progress was slow.

❦

Meanwhile, my brother, Mark, graduated from UC Berkeley with double bachelor's in psychology and religious studies. I flew out to California for the graduation ceremony. When I told Eric about the trip and I got ready to leave, he said kindly, "Call me if you need anything." I didn't tell him then, and in fact have never told him, but I really appreciated his concern and attention. I warmed to having friends, outside of Carter, in Houston now.

When I arrived in California, my mom, Mark, and I wandered the UC Berkeley campus and bookstore before the graduation ceremony. Mark was no longer a sweet and cute little boy, the curious tiny fellow who liked to make model ships and burn them in buckets. He towered over both of us, sporting the muscles and tattoos of a seasoned young Californian. But I saw a little bit of the brother I remembered in him.

When we glimpsed the small table near the underground bookstore at which a saleswoman took orders for class rings, I lit up. I went over to the covered table, picked up a form, and did quick calculations. I wanted to buy Mark one if I could afford it. I loved my own ring and remembered Michael's encouragement. If I moved forward with the idea, I wanted to make sure that I could afford whatever ring he wanted, no limits. After some quiet moments adding and subtracting, and considering how I might adjust my personal expenditures in the future if he wanted an emerald or diamond (especially the hefty emerald—yikes), I figured it could be done. Turning to Mark, I announced: "I would like to buy you a class ring if you want one."

He was lukewarm, not particularly interested.

"Seriously," I persisted, "I didn't want one either, but then Dad suggested I get it, and I'm so glad I did. It's different. It's important. It's a really neat feeling to have something physical—something that you can actually hold in your hand—to represent your graduation, your time in college. Pick any one you want. Any one at all! You can even get your name or a special phrase engraved inside."

Mom and I encouraged, cajoled, and eventually persuaded him to order one. The saleswoman described the different metal, design, and gem options to Mark. He listened carefully, taking so much time to consider the sample rings that Mom and I browsed the bookstore while we waited. Curious about his final decision, we nonetheless tried to avoid crowding him. His understated style tended to have flairs of creativity; he once covered a pair of jeans in calligraphic poetry with a Sharpie pen. The jeans looked like a piece of art when he was finished, expensive and designer. When he made his final choices and submitted the order, both Mom and

I were surprised. He chose a no-frills silver ring with no gemstone and a simple Latin inscription on the inside: *Servus servorum Dei*.

Servant of the servants of God. It had always been a meaningful expression to him, but in the years apart, I had forgotten about it completely. It was beautiful: A Roman Catholic pope's description of himself; an effort to emphasize the humility of service. Mark filled out his address and finished signing the forms, then rushed to join his classmates in the line to the side of the stage. During the ceremony my mom and I glimpsed Michael and Beth, who had flown in for the ceremony as well, but they sat in a different section of the outdoor theater. I felt a little ashamed. I hadn't seen Michael since I sent that awful letter, and didn't feel comfortable approaching him now—or welcome to—although suddenly I wished that we could all sit together.

My mom glanced over at them and away again, fine with the separation and, perhaps, even eager to maintain it. I watched Michael and Beth a bit longer. They sat together, facing the stage. They didn't look our way, but I was sure they saw us. I knew that if I approached Michael, my mom definitely wouldn't appreciate it. She'd made it clear that she didn't want to sit together. My heart bled while I looked at them. I suddenly resented my mother's presence next to me. She kept us apart. If I went to him, she would be alone. And he had Beth. My mom didn't have anybody. So I stayed, like a loyal dog, at her side, to protect and comfort her. And I wished that my family was a thing of joy, and not a constant battle, full of agony and balance.

The bay breezes were chilly and I began to think cold thoughts. I imagined the future, all of us on our deathbeds. I knew that the distance between us in this massive amphitheater right now would in the end seem unnecessary and rigid; it was tragic. As I looked across the curved stone benches, the whole space—supposed to be joyous and free with the warmth and fire of the future—felt like a bowl of ice and antiquity. My dad looked fragile and small. Even lonely. I felt a heart rush—regret—and looked away.

After the ceremony, all of the parties went our separate ways: Michael and Beth flew back to San Antonio. Mom returned to work just south of Berkeley. Mark wrapped up some graduation-related issues and would, over the course of the next few months, try to find meaningful work in the San Francisco Bay Area. I boarded the flight back to Houston and Post Oak. Work was going well; I liked the activity and challenges. But oh, my God, I was growing sick of Houston: everything from the pollution to the traffic, even the fact that the weather was so hot all the time. I loved exercising outside, but taking a walk in Houston felt like a chore.

To top it off, Carter and I hadn't been getting along very well; the constant daily tension was making both of us brittle and less compromising. I knew that I would need to get my own place soon; I needed, for the welfare of both of us (although he wouldn't see it that way), to break up with him. But it hurt. I loved him, and I knew he loved me. Moreover, I trusted him. It would be nice if things were different. But I just couldn't live with him. I needed to be alone, to figure things out, and have more harmony in my life.

꙳

Throughout the years traveling and working—including my time at Post Oak in Houston—I stayed in touch with Guy, my stepfather in California. Guy had two children himself. He was not as close to them as he would have liked to have been while they were growing up, and now they were grown and gone. He spoke from the side of my experience that I could not see.

"Tiffany, you should call him. He's your dad. He loves you and would love to hear from you."

"You don't understand," I protested. "I sent him a letter. It was pretty mean, and I don't think we're ever going to really talk again."

"You're his daughter. If you call him, he'll talk to you."

I saw the wisdom of his advice, but the silence and years were a big chasm. The whole situation felt like a web of confusion and half-truths. I was unable to decipher the reality of my relationship with my dad—where we stood now and how to make it better—yet incredibly intimidated at the thought of trying to heal or improve it. Any effort on my part was bound to be misconstrued. I thought sorting out the relationship would create more problems than just letting it sit and ferment. Guy's perspective, however, rested in my mind. On the nights when I was alone and quiet, I appreciated his staunch defense of Michael, although I didn't really understand it.

"Tiffany," he used to say, "you'll regret it if you don't talk to him. Give him a call."

But I didn't.

❧

Carter and I broke up in 2008, but remained friends. Toward the end of that year, Hurricane Ike hit Texas. I figured Houston was far enough inland that at least imminent death wasn't a huge concern, so I hunkered down. It's hard to describe what the air feels like before a hurricane—I suppose it's the barometric pressure dropping, in scientific terms, but the way that actually feels to someone who stands in the path of a storm, with a body of flesh and nerves that senses nature and danger, is another thing entirely. Everything was deathly still, and it was ominous; every little nerve I didn't know I had in my body trembled: *Something is coming.*

And then it came. At first there was no rain. Just wind and wind—and more wind. I heard the slapping and banging of things that don't normally move; early on, the shutters fell from the third story of the building. Then the rain came—in torrents, in floods—and water started pouring into my windows. As I saw more parts of the building falling down, and the water coming in, I realized that my apartment, my home, was not a shelter, and I started to comprehend how it all begins for the people who don't make it.

In the middle of the storm, electricity was already long gone. Light—a tiny, weak sample—came only from candles. My towels, which I had put by the windows, were soaked through completely; the carpet was now a giant puddle. When the storm was over and the sun finally appeared, trees, and thus electrical lines, were down everywhere. Suddenly more than a million people in Houston could not even get their morning cup of coffee. My friends and I survived; my car was still in one piece, but now I was smack-dab in the middle of a city full of crabby, scared, and unwashed people who may or may not have had access to a toilet that actually flushed.

It was awful—and it lasted for days.

The only truly unexpected and giant benefit was that I met more of my neighbors in those two days immediately afterward than I had in two years. People helped one another. They weren't isolated in their cars, or on their phones or computers or iPods. There was laughter and talking and walking around. In fact, in that regard, I actually felt like Hurricane Ike improved Houston. But when the electricity was reestablished, everyone went back into their televised cocoons and I reached a conclusion: I was through with Houston.

I didn't know how or where, but as soon as I could get a job somewhere else, I was moving. It was an easy choice, as I'd never really felt like I had a home anywhere; Houston was no exception. I'd had addresses and loved family members, yes, and I deeply cared for and supported Carter. But I felt I could only summon a faded tint of what others experienced in full color—namely, a sense of belonging and community. It was never fully satisfying and seemed even counterfeit. My mind twittered incessantly with a twisted, obsessive sense of impermanence. Circumstances would shift again—somehow, some way—but I constantly tried to anticipate and be one step ahead of life. Impending (and imagined) change sometimes made me quiver with anxiety.

Growing up, of course, I had moved around a lot. My mom and Mark were close, while I remained emotionally a little distance away and watched their fun. And Michael was always gone-here-gone. I don't know what exactly caused my deep-seated feeling of aloneness, but it enabled me to look at cities as a series of lily pads—with one about as good as the next. With no family as an anchor, I could leave and go anywhere. The economy was just starting to collapse, though, and unfortunately, an economic crisis is not generally considered a good time to relocate. I sat down to think about my options. I wanted three things in a city, whichever one ended up being my new home: a cooler climate, good public transportation (I was sick of driving!), and a center of industry that would either survive, or be insulated against, the downturn.

I pulled out a map and evaluated the United States with new eyes: Where did I want to be? I drew a line across the country that went straight through Houston. Nothing south of that. I crossed out California: Been there, done that. I crossed out New York: too crazy. After scratching and marking for a while, I identified five cities that sounded viable: Boston, Seattle, Baltimore, Chicago, and Washington, DC. I was born in Washington, DC, but I didn't remember it; beyond that, I had not been to any of them.

Okay, I thought, staring purposefully at the map. *So now what?*

Looking for jobs in all of them would waste effort. I decided I would visit each city on a weekend trip, see as much as I could, and then choose my favorite. Over the course of the following days and weeks, I talked to everybody I knew outside of work to get as much information about those cities as possible, while trying to keep it quiet that I was looking to move. I didn't want to lose the job I already had. The only work colleague in whom I confided was Anna, confident that she would support me and not inadvertently let the cat out of the bag. During my research—all of the conversations and e-mails—an acquaintance of mine who traveled a lot said, "You want to stay away from Baltimore, but Washington, DC, is great, and the people there are awesome. Chicago's a nice city but the winters are epic."

Ew, I thought. I had not considered that a city might be too cold. I scratched Chicago off the list. Snow was pretty in pictures and when one was skiing; I didn't want to slog through it on my way to work. Baltimore stayed on the list; it was close to DC. That could even be the first trip: two birds with one stone. Motivation and inspiration coursed through me like invigorating lifeblood. Work was an unknown, but I knew that I *wanted* to move. I felt great! When Carter and I met for dinner one evening, I told him my plan. He just stared at me for a moment. "You mean you're going to move to a city you've never been to, get a job, and leave Houston? Just like that?"

"Well . . . I think it'll be harder than *just like that* . . . but yes, that's the plan."

"That's crazy."

"Well," I replied, undeterred, "it's what I'm doing."

A few weekends later, I landed in the DC area. Baltimore proved the acquaintance correct: It *was* rough. The Inner Harbor was pleasant, with tourists and businesspeople milling around, but other parts of the city were dilapidated. I removed Baltimore from consideration. Washington, DC, was next, nestling in my mind like the green grass on the other side of the fence, so I headed down I-95 to visit.

When I arrived, I called Anna's aunt Sarah first thing. She ran a firm in the DC area and Anna had put me in touch with her. Sarah suggested meeting for lunch. We met at Rosa Mexicana, a restaurant near the Gallery Place Metro station, and talked about working and living in the city. Full of wisdom and insight, Sarah shared advice without reserve. She took time to really understand my goals in possibly moving up to DC, and helped me figure out the best courses of action to look for jobs and set up interviews.

"You'll love it!" she said. "I really hope you can move up here!"

After lunch, she took me for a tour of the city and the major attractions: the Capitol, the White House, the Washington Monument, the Pentagon, and the beautiful George Washington Parkway that winds its way through grassy expanses, right across the Potomac River from the District and its famous cherry trees. I was in awe! The old town homes, myriad restaurants, and extraordinary monuments in a giant parklike setting were all chock-full of history. The city pulsed as if it were the heartbeat of the world. The weather, the people, the scenery: Everything was perfect. There was no need to see Boston or Seattle. I wanted to live in Washington, DC.

THE DISTRICT

Ireturned to Houston with a new focus. Each evening, when I got home from work, I geared all my energy into finding a job in DC. That was no easy feat: I lived more than a thousand miles away. Employers, understandably, wanted to meet me in person. I planned intense trips to interview, with three or four meetings a day spread all over Washington every day, for three or four days—and then I'd fly back to Houston and Post Oak. I said yes to every opportunity to interview, grabbing at any chance.

All of the expenses—hotels, flights, transportation, and food—terrorized my bank account. Finally, I had almost nothing left. I returned to Intercontinental Airport in Houston, fresh from my latest excursion to Washington, and, as I picked up my car from the economy lot, considered the financial situation. Waiting at the intersection to take the freeway home, I thought, *I have enough money for one more trip and next month's rent—and that's it. Maybe I should just cut my losses and let this go.* My heart seethed with frustration at the idea. The wide Texas sky and tall trees nearby framed my vision as I sat at the light. The only other car at the intersection was right in front of me—and its license plate looked unusual.

That's not Texas; where the heck is that license plate from?

I inched my car closer to get a better look.

It was from Washington, DC.

Now, that's weird.

I had never seen a DC license plate in Texas; in fact, DC is so small I felt a tiny percentage of the cars in the world must have DC tags. *Why is it here now? Is that a sign?* Just a few days before, Anna had said, *There's no such thing as coincidence.* I didn't want to let go of the dream. I wanted it too badly. If I was going down, I decided, then by God I was going down in flames.

When I got home, I bought tickets for one more trip. As before, I interviewed like mad, made unscheduled stops by the offices of the senior executives of organizations I wanted to work for, brazenly interrupting their assistants to make my case. I knocked on the doors of representatives in Congress, talked to people on the trains, even answered classified ads.

And nothing happened.

The last interview I'd had, of seven of that trip, was with a contractor for a government agency just north of DC. It had gone well (I thought), but all I heard were crickets afterward. That evening, I went to bed late, exhausted and gazing blankly into space, utterly miserable. I'd tried—and lost. I'd put all of myself into making the move, done everything I knew to do, and came up short. The next day was my last full day in Washington. There was nothing left. No interviews scheduled. No long shots in the pipeline. No money for more trips. Every opportunity was empty. I was empty. I had no job in DC; no one was interested in me. I'd be stuck in Houston forever. The next morning I woke up and, feeling the blankets around me, remembered I was in DC. My mind clicked on: *No job.*

Ah, hell.

Then I inhaled and threw off the covers. "Well," I announced to myself, "since everything else is a complete wash, might as well go see something new."

I put on a pants suit (just in case I got the wild notion to stop by another poor, unsuspecting person's office) and strode drearily out the door. I got on the Metro train and rode into downtown DC, deciding on a morning game plan. It had to be a cheap one, whatever it was. I opted for a pumpkin muffin. That, at least, was affordable.

I had discovered a fantastic little bakery called Firehook in Dupont Circle and loved their pumpkin muffins. I bought one and perched at the tiny bar. Watching DC stroll by, I sat, weary, on the bar stool. The little pumpkin treat was a comfort—and I was hungry—but it lasted only so long. I finished, threw the napkin away, and, as I was heading out the door, my phone rang.

When I answered, a lady responded, but all I heard was, "agency," and ". . . would like to offer you the position."

Are you kidding me?

I tried to play it cool, but inside I was jumping for joy! I was to serve as the executive assistant to the leader of a scientific division. *Fantastic!* I didn't know anything about the division's specialty to speak of, but I didn't need to. I needed to know how to manage time and be organized—and that I could do. I hung up the phone in a state of sheer ecstasy and, moments later, reality sank in: *Oh, my God.*

I've got to find a place. Today.

I stood in the middle of the busy sidewalk, just thinking. When I talked with Sarah, she suggested that Dupont Circle and Woodley Park were good neighborhoods around Metro stations. I decided to walk in concentric circles around those stations and stop at every apartment complex that was open. I didn't have time to be picky. I had approximately five hours, on foot, to find housing in DC—or else take my chances getting a place remotely. I needed to take whatever looked clean, safe, and affordable.

My favorite apartment, which I considered for a nanosecond until I actually viewed it, had hardwood floors frozen in a strange undulation that resembled the surface of an agitated sea. It would hold a coffee table, but only pitched forward at a very precarious angle. I revamped my expectations and requirements to reflect more basic standards: flat floors and no strange smells—pee, trash, or otherwise. Fortunately, prospects improved just in the nick of time, right when I was emotionally and physically spent. Following a tall leasing agent to see the next apartment, I hauled myself slowly up the few stairs, as if my body were luggage. But as soon as I saw the elevated ceilings and pleasant layout of the small studio apartment, I knew it was the one. With two minutes to spare before the building management office closed for the day—and once I handed over a bigger check than I had ever written before—the place was mine.

Right by a Metro station.

Perfect.

~∙~

Colleagues took over my projects at Post Oak as I transitioned. During my last weeks in Houston, I wrapped up a commitment to help Anna and her colleagues at the archdiocese host a large annual footrace to raise funds for inner-city schools. The race, called "Steps for Students," had necessitated months of preparation. The expertise and dedication of the board members, all community volunteers, helped address a massive number of essential concerns and made race day seem effortless. After all of the work invested, I felt a deep loyalty to the project. I wrote in my journal the night before the race:

> *I told Anna I would meet her at the 59 Diner at 3:30 a.m. before the Steps for Students run tomorrow. She told me she was going to get to the race at 4:30 a.m. [to set up] and I exclaimed, WHAT?! I had no idea she was getting there so early and felt that my friend shouldn't have to do all that in the dark and cold all by herself. So I told her I was going. And around about 3:00 a.m. tomorrow, I do believe I'll regret that. Ha, ha!*

I went. The red-eye breakfast at the 59 Diner was fantastic. We drank coffee, and our sleepy laughter and inane comments got louder. We ran ourselves ragged with preparations at the race site that morning with another archdiocesan staffer named John. The race itself went well. College athletes sprinted, parents trotted, and small children bumbled down the course in a smiling cacophony of support. Turnout was higher than expected.

I felt happy.

At Post Oak, I'd developed confidence in my own ability to manage projects; I felt rewarded and significant when I saw our work around the city. I would miss it! And Carter. He was such a strong and sincere man. Even though I didn't believe we were meant to be together forever, I knew he would be there if I needed help. Carter and Post Oak had taught me how to trust and engage in life. I was less hesitant—almost healed in a way. Maybe I still had a scab somewhere in my soul, but at least I wasn't bleeding profusely.

When I got back home early that afternoon, I fell onto my bed, completely exhausted. The morning had been active and childishly fun. Resting for the first time all day, I abruptly felt sad. I was leaving all of this . . . and soon. I would miss Houston. I had to leave all of my friends, my great boss, my coworkers. I suddenly wanted a feeling of connection—with *something*. I thought of Michael, how much he liked adventuring around new places, how he sought out novel experiences to taste everything that life had to offer. He might understand why I was doing this. He might believe that it was cool that I was moving back to where I was born. In a moment of impulse and courage, I decided to take Guy's advice: I'd call Michael and at least be nice.

The mattress gave way underneath me as I sat up, hunched over, and dialed the phone. I knew the numbers. The phone rang.

"Hello?" my dad answered. His familiar tones dragged me—always—back to places I'd left long ago.

"Hey, Dad," I said, strangely aware of the bulky furniture around me. It seemed heavy and contrasted oddly, in my mind, with my own voice. The sounds I made were wispy, ineffective, as if I were tossing something to him that would never make it. A child throwing a feather back to its owner in the sky.

"Hi, honey!" His voice sounded surprised, happiness mixed with some guardedness.

Stilted and awkward, the conversation sputtered. Outside of the problems we had had, and our extensive lack of communication, I suddenly wanted him to enjoy the DC announcement. I had really good news for once! I'd found this unknown strength in myself to pursue my dreams. I was doing things a little against the grain, even if other people thought they were odd, because I believed in them. *Did he like that?*

"Oh, that's great, Tiffany! Congratulations. You'll love DC!"

He recommended dozens of museums and the Civil War battlefields nearby in Virginia, Maryland, and Pennsylvania. He reminisced a little about when we all lived at Fort Meade together and (sure enough) when I was born at Walter Reed in DC. But that was it. He never mentioned the letter. Nothing was resolved. Whatever churned in the moat between us was still submerged and alive. His life was in San Antonio and mine was elsewhere—soon to be a lot farther elsewhere.

When we hung up, I felt like we were strangers again.

So much for connection. I sat on my bed, staring mindlessly out my window into the sunny distance, not really seeing the moving picture of midday in Texas. It seemed as if there was dirtiness between me and my dad that needed to be cleaned. But I didn't know how. If I could just make the black white, and the far near, I would have felt so *free*. Looking back now, I could have been the one to do it—it would have, I believe, required simple honesty—but I was too young, too confused, and too afraid.

So I slumped over in a disappointed heap and slept.

❧

When I actually moved to DC, I realized Sarah was right: Washington was a world apart from Houston, from what people wore to how they behaved. It took time for me to get accustomed to the new city scene, the Metro train system, and a lifestyle built around the presence of government. Elitism was much more acceptable in Washington than I expected: Embassy cars parked in fire lanes. Police rerouted entire streets because somebody was deemed the most important person within a certain radius. DC was full of kings, but as the Italian proverb goes, when the game is over, the king and the pawn go back into the same box.

Fortunately, DC was also full of cool people, individuals who, even if they wore mismatched socks and scuffed-up shoes, paid direct attention to others and demonstrated intelligence and thoughtful care. I did not want to get mixed up in the spiritual trap of not caring about others; I wanted to protect the budding sense of authenticity within me—it made me feel happy. I had once heard that, in order to support decisions you make in life, you need to surround yourself with people who encourage, uplift, and empower you. I'd never consciously tried to do that, but in DC, I applied that principle almost religiously.

After about a year of learning curves, feeling comfortable now in the new city and at my job, I decided to make a trip back to Houston to see Anna. It had been too long! I wanted to laugh with my friend again. I arranged for a flight back and told her I'd meet her at Starbucks.

❧

When I arrived at the Shepherd Avenue Starbucks in Houston, I sat down to wait until Anna got there, when suddenly I remembered that my phone was on silent and she might be trying to call. Pulling it out of my purse, I gawked in shock. Within the last half hour alone, my dad had called once, Mark twice, and my mom just a few minutes ago. Something was wrong.

At that moment, Anna arrived. I told her about the missed calls, and dialed my mom while we walked to her car.

When my mom answered, her voice was strained. "Tiffany, your dad has been diagnosed with stage-four intestinal cancer."

The earth reeled; everything left my mind: *What?*

"It's very advanced." My mom spoke directly, as if she were trying to make hearing the bad news easier by delivering it as clearly as possible. "He's at the hospital right now, about to have emergency surgery. They don't know if he's going to live."

No!

Impossible.

Anna heard everything and looked at me, bewildered and concerned. She turned off Shepherd Avenue into a parking lot. My body was so full of concentrated adrenaline that, as Anna pulled in and I dialed my dad, I experienced a shock of distraction: *Why on earth are we pulling into Taco Bell?*

The phone was ringing.

Beth answered. She was crying and repeated what my mom had just said.

Old news! Old news! my mind screamed. *Let me talk to him!* My personality, in moments of crisis, demanded action. But I'd learned to temper and rein in my natural impatience. Beth was intensely upset and needed to communicate. I tried to breathe in patience, to listen to all that she told me. I told myself she would pass the phone along if Michael was about to be wheeled into surgery that second. *She is a parent too, after all. She understands. She wouldn't let me miss him. . . .*

If can't talk to him now, I might never talk to him again.

"He's been feeling bad for some time," Beth was saying, her voice choked with sobs, "but when he went to the doctor they didn't find anything wrong. This is all so surprising! Even he didn't expect cancer!"

I became hyperaware of everything I could feel and see. While Beth talked, I sat in the passenger seat of Anna's vehicle. Suddenly I felt the coolness of the door handle. I didn't realize that I had been holding it. I looked up through the windshield and was peripherally aware of Anna in the driver's seat. My conscious mind, presiding over the court of my wild emotions, could not make sense of the madness. I checked out. Suddenly, I noticed the small, unassuming trees behind the Taco Bell.

What beautiful branches! I inexplicably thought.

Then my lungs started to constrict. I was terrified my dad was going to die before I got to talk to him. Finally, Beth passed the phone over.

My dad came on the line, sounding very weak. "Hi, Tiffany."

The years vaporized in an instant, and I was a kid again.

"Hi, Dad!" I said softly. "How are you feeling? Beth just told me that you're sick. . . ."

"Yes, they've discovered that I have cancer." He elaborated on the details and spoke very matter-of-factly about the surgery, as if facts were the steady things that could save him. As he spoke, I could hear the fear in his voice—and the good-bye.

"I'll call you when I get out of surgery. And, Tiffany, if I don't make it through this surgery . . . I want you to know that I'm very proud of you. And I love you very much."

I lost my tenuous grip on control, and teardrops rolled down my cheeks. *Stupid things!* I could feel him forcing all of his love and energy into his words, as if he could somehow encapsulate all that he felt into them. *How do you speak words that will last someone for the rest of their life?*

"I love you too, Dad. . . ."

The line went quiet, but I didn't hang up. Then I heard his voice say softly, "It's okay to hang up now, Tiffany. I love you."

"Okay, Dad. I love you too."

I hung up, in the stupor of shock, and cried.

I-10 WESTBOUND

When I calmed down, I stared quietly at the phone's dark screen and its miniature buttons. *How can life change so quickly?* I pictured my dad hundreds of miles away, nervously being wheeled into the operating room. He didn't know whether he'd come out alive. I didn't know whether he'd be alive in an hour.

"I am so, so sorry, Tiffany," Anna said slowly. "We can go to San Antonio tonight or tomorrow morning."

It took me a moment to process her words.

"What?" I asked, stuttering and confused. Then her meaning dawned on me: "Oh, no, Anna, absolutely not. I do not want to ruin your weekend! I'll go by myself. I'll rent a car."

It was Anna's turn to look surprised. "What? No! That's *silly*! I'm your friend. This is what friends do! I'm going to take you to San Antonio to see your dad."

"Anna, listen. My dad and I haven't always gotten along. And, well, it's just not going to be easy."

"I'm not here for easy, Tiffany. I'm here for you."

I brushed away tears and sniffled. "Thank you for being such a good friend."

Beth called me late in the afternoon. Dad was still alive. The surgery was done, but not exactly successful. The cancer was so far advanced that the doctors couldn't do anything to help. There wasn't enough left of his intestines for them to discriminate between what was healthy and what was not.

"You could probably come to San Antonio to say good-bye," Beth said. "I don't know if he'll be alive when you get here, though. They've only given him a couple days to live. We're spending the night in the hospital tonight," she continued, "so the doctors can monitor him, but there's nothing they can do for him here, so we're going to get him discharged tomorrow so he can come home."

Home? The word sounded to me, at that very moment, so bizarre. Where is home when you are dying?

I thanked Beth and hung up. Anna and I spent the evening coordinating and making plans. I canceled other meetings I'd arranged. Mark, out in California, was able to get a flight from San Francisco to San Antonio moments after he found out. We were to pick him up at the San Antonio airport the next day. This would be the first time that both Mark and I would be with our dad—all three of us together—in more than four years. It was remarkable. None of us had worked very hard to maintain the reality or feeling of a family. Mark and I never really spoke about Michael. We shared him as a father, as a past; he was like a superstar, simultaneously familiar and unknown, who had strolled throughout our lives on the red carpet of kinship.

Anna and I got adjoining rooms at a hotel near Interstate 10, and the wake-up call came in what felt like the middle of the night. I hardly slept; my mind howled with memories and dreams. I staggered upright, bleary-eyed, and knocked on Anna's room. She was already awake and ready to go. We got on the road to San Antonio within fifteen minutes. The long miles passed quickly, first under the fading stars and then under the rising sun.

Driving to see Dad, I thought. *It's just like normal.*
And yet it's not this time.
Because Dad is dying.

It was spring in Texas and the wildflowers were in full bloom. A little extra color graced everything: Some fields were explosions of blue and yellow. I had heard that some people hate the months and the seasons in which their loved ones pass, as if every successive year brings them back, timeless, to the moment of parting. *What a beautiful time to die. I don't want to hate every spring.* I pleaded with God, *Couldn't he stay a little longer? Heaven can't be much prettier than Texas in the spring.* I remembered times with my dad like a series of snapshots—my life, his life, our moments together. And now all of those years apart, full of anger, seemed like a massive, despicable, and unforgivable crime.

We arrived in San Antonio before noon and dropped by the hospital to see Beth. Michael was in with doctors and would be for a couple more hours. Anna and I left, grabbed some food at Madhatters (my suggestion), and picked up some treats and flowers for my dad at H-E-B Central Market. On a whim, I picked up a brightly colored miniature piñata—a donkey, of all things—for his hospital room. I thought the colors would be cheery and help him feel better. But as I stood in the checkout line with Anna, the garish paper of the piñata disgusted me. *So this is my attempt at consolation and gratitude?* He had done so much for me—helping me move to San Antonio and supporting me through high school and college—that the piñata seemed almost insulting in return. But it was colorful, and I couldn't afford much else, certainly not the thousands of roses I would like to have offered, so the donkey, in all its fiesta glory, came with us.

We picked Mark up at the airport. He seemed on guard, as if he had used the travel time to steel himself against intimacy and vulnerability. But maybe I was projecting; that is what I had done. He spotted our vehicle almost immediately and jumped in. We headed to the hospital, discussing the latest updates. Mark was focused and businesslike; I hadn't seen him in more than a year and would have liked to catch up, but his demeanor did not invite conversation. When we did talk, it was in an isolated, heavy manner—the same way that raindrops drip, after the rain has stopped falling, from a patio roof. The mild but indispensable comfort for both of us remained in the familiar tones of each other's voices—but often the car was just silent. I was feeling too much to talk, alternately swept by emotion and the tiniest of practical matters (like, we would need to get gas soon); Mark, tired and hungry, appeared to be just trying to make it through the ride to see Dad, and Anna stayed respectfully silent, refusing to infringe on our thoughts.

Anna dropped the two of us off at the hospital and went to find a parking place. We entered and the corridors felt almost abandoned, with a dusty smell, as if we'd stepped back in time a few decades. We could hear voices but didn't see a single person. I carried a bag of cookies and the colorful piñata; Mark had the other bag of cookies. We found our dad's hospital room by ourselves and appeared in his doorway together.

I saw him before he saw us; he was looking at Beth, on the other side of the bed. *Oh, my God.* He looked so thin and frail. He looked like death, like he was waiting for it, even wishing for it. *He isn't supposed to look that way! What has gone wrong with life?* Propped up on pillows in the hospital bed, he was a fossil of himself, moving his jaw in a strange, repetitive motion. He turned his head slowly to the doorway.

Beth had not told him that we would be coming, in order to keep it a surprise. When he saw us, his eyes lit up and his face broke into a huge smile. The jaw movements ceased.

"Tiffany! Mark!"

"Hi, Dad!" I entered the room with Mark, forcing myself to smile. Beth and her oldest son were sitting on either side of him, the three of them in a loose triangle as Mark and I came in. I wanted to be strong and positive for everyone, especially *him*, but suddenly even the tiniest stimuli felt painfully powerful.

The dark room reminded me of a cavern. There was a sense of passing into a vast chamber, as if the room didn't stop at the walls. My father's hospital bed was in the center, an angular pedestal that held him up in linens, under a single light, for everyone to view: a fragile artifact. *Not that body. He is so much more than that body.*

Michael beamed, made small movements with his hands. Reached out to hug us. He started to shake and then let go into a flood of happy tears. I looked at him for a split second, could barely manage the strength. I wished to see a steady, reassuring presence. I desperately wanted to comprehend him and not ever have that knowledge flit or tumble away from me, obsolete and useless. I wanted *him* to last for *always.*

Mark and I moved awkwardly around everyone, through the greetings and into Michael's broad smiles. He overflowed with joy.

I struggled to be positive. And calm.

"We brought you some treats and picked up this little piñata to brighten your day," I said lightheartedly. I smiled and held up the piñata in an exaggerated presentation. As I set it down on the table at his eye level, I glimpsed Beth out of the corner of my eye. She was smiling, through tears, at Michael.

"Oh, Mark . . . oh, Tiffany"—he was crying—"I am so happy to see you!"

Mark approached the bed and leaned down, his huge, healthy shape a stark contrast to Michael's weak form. Michael put his arms out for a hug and held on. And on. And on.

I knew it must have been tearing Mark apart inside. But he didn't quake and, when Michael let him go with a radiant smile, my brother straightened up, a tall wall of back and shoulders in the middle of the room. I walked closer to the hospital bed; Mark retreated toward the back wall. I didn't want to hug my dad. Every bit of affection and love seemed to certify that he was leaving us. But I bent down, closed the space, and pressed his frail body against my own. My heart lurched inside of me.

Dad. You are not supposed to look like this.

Now that I had him in my arms, I didn't want to let go. *You're not supposed to look like this!*

The doctor popped his head into the room in a kindly, calm manner and said he was "just wrapping up the paperwork."

It struck me as the most absurd, idiotic thing I had ever heard.

Anger suddenly surged through me. I released my dad and turned my head to see this man. He was young, handsome. Smiled at me, obviously trying to make things easier.

I hated bureaucracy.

But when I turned back to my dad, he looked almost perky, talking with Mark. The flash of anger disappeared. I perched on a creaky metal stool and listened to their conversation—familiar, casual—and chimed in occasionally. I sat there in the room and leaned forward with my elbows on my knees. I wanted to give my father the best of life. To forget the problems; to heal every injury and pain in the blink of an eye. I wanted to wash everything with forgiveness and gratitude. To be at peace and, quite simply, to offer him all of the flowers in the world.

DAD

Later that day, after he got back home from the hospital and settled in at Beth's house on Magnolia Avenue, Michael and I sat alone in the dining room. The others were in another room, and Michael was resting in a chair near the end of the large farm-style table. I felt sad and unsure of what to say, how to give or receive comfort.

I had brought my journal to San Antonio and abruptly had an idea. I liked it when friends and loved ones wrote in my journals; often I would go back and reread what they wrote years later. It always felt like a precious snapshot of the moment and who they were.

"Dad, would you like to write in my journal?"

He lit up, as much as he could, given all of the drugs. "I'd love to!"

I sat down, purposeful and diligent, on the hardwood floor next to his chair. Michael picked up a pen and looked at the book. There was a small heart sticker on the most recent page I'd written. He smiled slowly, seeming to make an enormous effort just to concentrate, his eyes sometimes closing against his will.

"I'll start where you ended, by the little heart. . . ."

He started writing. He wrote some letters twice, and put all of his power into forming each one. He stopped again—and again— just trying to focus and breathe. Once I thought he might have even fallen asleep. He was taking so much medication that he could not function well. I cried silently, determined to hide it.

Alert with a sudden desperation, I searched for any idea that would help me connect with him, something that I could hold on to after he was gone, to feel that he was still a part of my life. I remembered a story about two people who shared a special symbol; it became a magical connection for them. I wondered momentarily about us maybe sharing a sign—even glancing over at him as he wrote, as if inspecting him could help me predict his reaction to the idea. His head was bent down as he focused. Dad. A Catholic man from the Deep South. His closed posture prompted insecurity to clamor within me.

Michael.

He would probably think it was hogwash. He might not like the idea. A conservative upbringing and years in the U.S. Army did not normally make one's mind a fertile ground for ideas like astrology, acupuncture, or the dead talking to the living through signs embedded like guideposts throughout life. I wanted to ask him, though. I desperately wanted something extraordinary between us, something miraculous. So what if he thought it was silly? It was worth asking. I forced myself to speak.

"Dad," I said slowly. "I heard a story once of a man whose mom died. They were very close, and before she died, they agreed on a symbol that she would use to show that she was around him. They agreed on a white bird, and after she died white birds appeared at really peculiar or pivotal moments in his life. I thought . . . that it might be cool if we had a symbol like that. Would you . . . would you like that?"

When you're gone.

My heart shrank back into a little cave; I was afraid that he would laugh at me.

"Oh, yes!" he replied.

I sat up straighter, delighted. "What would you want as the symbol?"

There was no hesitation at all: "A shamrock." He spoke with so much force and confidence that for a moment it did not seem like he was dying.

Never in a million years would I have suspected that that would be his answer. I hadn't thought of my old high school mascot in years. But it was clearly very real and significant to him. It seemed almost like our life in San Antonio was still current; it was so alive in his heart! The shamrock was the sign of our year together. And it was important to him. *How perfect is that?!* I looked up at him and beamed.

It was settled. I didn't often see a bunch of shamrock symbols, except maybe on St. Patrick's Day. They would be rare enough to actually make me believe he was really around if I saw one. I wondered how he'd pull that off . . . and how he'd feel in heaven when he was doing it. And quietly, a subversive afterthought: *I wonder if he'll ever actually show me a shamrock.*

As we sat together I tried to remember every tiny detail of the room, the air, and his presence. The sun came through the cream-colored lace curtains, not as a direct, unbroken beam but diffused. Ethereal. The dark wooden table and the linens on the windowsill stuck out in my mind. They were so solid, so domestic and real. My dad seemed like the most featherlight thing in the room. Lighter than the sunshine. He was so incredibly thin. But his spirit was breathtaking. It emanated from him with actual force. It seemed like the weaker his body got, the stronger his spirit became. Nothing about his outward appearance suggested strength; in fact, his shoulders and head were hunched over a little in pain. In a photograph, he would have looked plagued and vulnerable. However, sitting next to him in person was a completely different experience, like looking at a photo of a swimming pool versus diving into one.

In life, some people can almost magically make you feel better. You grin just seeing them smile, the way the wrinkles around their eyes scrunch up in joy when they look at you, when they laugh. They lift you up. They make you think of funny things, of better days. Moments with them throb with wildness and wealth. Laughter and contentment wash over you—you, the wanderer looking for water. I have met such people, who were themselves the best kind of gift, but I'd never experienced anything quite like this.

A halo of extraordinary peace surrounded him, even though I knew he was in pain. His calmness soothed my heart and turned my mind to higher things. Being near him made me think of God and heaven; and the world I thought I knew. All of the conflict in the world seemed so petty and ridiculous. There was—clearly—so much more. I suddenly remembered an odd thing: the old statue *Winged Victory*. That sculpture is missing the head and arms, and

Michael's presence similarly did not feel propelled by mind—its endless wants and needs and fears—or oriented to manipulating the world.

He, dying, next to me, was all Heart—unassailable, soothing; a loving force striding forward that could take flight at any time. Power and serenity flowed from him, outward from a hidden fount. Not power over anything or anyone, but power from within. Innate. Transformative.

It struck me then: *He isn't dying.*

He is becoming.

I wished for the minutes to last in that dining room. I berated myself for all the days that I'd been with him and not comprehended how rare and special our moments together could be. Even now, I didn't know exactly where we stood, either in relation to each other or to God, but I knew that, whatever we had between us, it was far more powerful than I ever realized.

Lord, please help me appreciate this present moment, with him, right now. Please help me to remember all of the details and feelings— the truth of it—later. When he's gone, I'd be willing to buy this house if Beth ever wanted to sell it, just to sit in this dining room and remember. I listened to him breathe, and to my own breathing. I took a slow, full breath and felt the air fill my lungs. He continued to write in my journal.

Soon, Michael closed his eyes and said, "Tiffany, I can't . . . I'm having trouble writing. I'm trying to write, 'It was more than I ever could have hoped for,' but I can't. I'm having trouble thinking. . . ."

I looked down; my eyes got hot. He spoke so softly that it was difficult for me to hear. His strength, mental and physical, was trickling away. I reached for the pen that he held out to me and noticed his hand was weak and trembling. My heart skipped a beat—*he is leaving me already!*—but I took the pen.

"It's okay, Dad. I'll write that down for you." I listened to him speak softly again in my mind, picked out each individual word. I wanted to get the words down verbatim. I wrote as he bowed his head. He tried to breathe deeply.

"Thank you, honey," he said on an exhale.

When I finished, he asked for some help to stand up. He needed to go to the bathroom. The intestinal cancer caused him a lot of problems eliminating, and constant pain. Beth took him into the bathroom. I knew they would be in there a long time. I had to get some food for dinner for everyone that night, so I lifted myself off the floor. As I heard the water faucet and muted voices through the door, I saw the journal on the table. I leaned forward and picked it up. I felt the soft leather, the heft of its weight, and I looked down to read my father's words—the words he'd struggled to write through the medication and the pain:

> *Saturday*
> *17 Appril*
> *19:43*
> *Hello Tiff—What a nice*
> *surpprisse to*
> *get to see both you + Mark*
> *today. It was more than I*
> *I coreuld… [illegible]*

And then, in my own handwriting:

> *It was more than I ever could have hoped for.*

MOVING BOXES

L ate that night, when Beth and Michael had gone to bed at Magnolia, Mark and I spent quiet hours at Allensworth, going through all of Michael's old things while Anna slept in the back bedroom. We didn't talk very much; both of us were satisfied to just think on our own and know the other one was close. Michael still had a box room, and accumulated clutter was scattered haphazardly about. No one had cleaned that house in months; some boxes contained several decades' worth of his life: Photos of unfamiliar people by the dozens in military uniforms, clearly friends and colleagues neither Mark nor I had ever known. Financial files. Announcements from Catholic churches for food drives, fund-raisers, and special events. In the attic, when I peeked inside, there were boxes of Playmobil toys.

I had forgotten about the collections of toys. Up until that moment I had been precariously balanced. I could view the paperwork (bills, letters) and items (camouflage jackets, military medals) from his career and daily life with efficient composure. But when I saw the Playmobil boxes, I was yanked within by dark regret. I felt as if he were a child, vulnerable and isolated, all alone in the world and just trying to be happy, and that somehow I had failed him in the blackest way possible. Not just failed him, but been one of those vicious people who caused him pain and suffering. I pushed the feeling aside.

I will deal with that later.

I folded up the attic ladder and closed the door. Mark and I perused the remaining boxes slowly in separate rooms, as there simply wasn't enough room for two people to work together in one. Occasionally there was a shuffle and footsteps on the old floorboards. Sometimes one of us would raise our voice and announce, through the walls, a rediscovered relic from childhood.

I moved a box to the side and pulled another down right in front of me. Boxes shifted against one another with a distinctive sound: dry and crisp. The sound of change. Some of the stuff inside was so familiar, from thick brown ceramic plates to musty, wrinkled clothes. I remembered so much, including the button-down shirts that he used to wear: shirts in bright colors or odd patterns that nevertheless looked sophisticated when he wore them. I knelt by the large side panel of one box and started inspecting the contents. I was about midway through when I glimpsed the bottom and paused.

There was a small container. It looked almost like trash, but something about the tarnished object and the refined angles inside looked more valuable than junk. There was a suggestion of art and meaning in it, a hint through the bent and dusty plastic. Opening it up, I scattered the contents—military pins, small souvenirs, and some items I couldn't identify—on the floor. Tinkles and clinks, then silence. In the debris before me, one of the items looked very familiar, but I couldn't place it.

Then it dawned on me.

Oh, my God. It's the necklace. . . .

He'd kept his half.

Hours later, sleep would not come.

I lay awake on the dining room floor, wrapped up in an old blanket like a miserable burrito. Mark and Anna were asleep in the adjoining rooms, Mark in the living room and Anna in my old bedroom. The blanket felt soft and warm, even though it smelled a bit musty. Silence and safety shrouded everything. It seemed as though the entire world were at rest. The only sound in the house was the gentle hum of the refrigerator in the tiny, empty kitchen.

Earlier that evening, while sifting through the boxes, I chose to keep some items as mementos of my father. They were in a small pile nearby. Mark had picked out some things as well and piled them neatly next to mine. I glanced over at both piles occasionally, feeling grateful that Mark was here. The two little piles were like our two hearts and memories; they looked tiny and vulnerable. They made me want to protect Mark, although from what, I didn't know. I took a deep breath and looked away, reminiscing once more about all the wonderful days in San Antonio with Michael. And I kept thinking, again and again, as if it were the chorus in a never-ending song: *I should have kept my half.*

TEXAS AGGIE, HOMEWARD BOUND

Anna offered to stay in San Antonio as long as necessary. But I wouldn't ask that of her—and couldn't do it anyway. My boss in DC had been more than accommodating, but I didn't want to take advantage of that generosity. I felt like I had to return to Washington, but I still agonized. I could quit my job and stay in San Antonio with Michael. Over the weekend, he had already outlived the doctors' predictions. I didn't want to say good-bye and leave him. It would be like turning my back on a gift from God: the gift of more time with him. How would I feel back in my apartment in DC, knowing that he was still alive in San Antonio, but only for a little longer . . . and that I would never see him again?

But Michael himself became forceful in the issue. He encouraged me to return to Washington. He said it was okay, that he was so happy to see me, and that he felt so grateful to God. "You need to go live your life. Don't quit your job and give things up just because of me. I'm okay now—and when I die, I'll be okay. Beth's taking good care of me. Go—go and live your life. I love you so much, and I am so, so happy for this time together."

I saw the sincerity in his face and sensed it in his words, the way he leaned forward slightly and looked at me intensely. But I did not want to agree—it was too much like the perfect excuse, the ideal reason to run away from him. I believed I should shoulder his pain and help until I wasted into something that could no longer bring joy or benefit; to die with him in a way. I felt as if that were my duty. But he meant it. He spoke his words as if they were an order to be obeyed.

With a heavy heart, and not completely convinced it was the best decision, I went. Mark remained; he would stay another few days.

During the trip back, I kept returning to one idea: I had a lot to learn. Everything that had happened, including the feeling now as I got farther and farther from him, reminded me of a friendly old neighbor we'd had in central California. The neighbor lived on the cul-de-sac near Guy's old house. Her daughter had been critically injured in a horrific car accident. As soon as she heard about the accident, the woman had rushed to the hospital. Her daughter was still alive. She held her daughter's hand, and continued to hold it, as the girl died in the emergency room.

Our neighbor said to me later, "I could not let go of her hand. After all the years . . . she is my daughter. I could not let go. They had to take my hand out of hers."

The woman had turned to me and asked softly, as if I could possibly know the answer, "When do you let go?"

I sat quietly in the passenger seat as Anna drove down the interstate. Tears rolled down my cheeks as I looked through the window at the stars. Finally, as the false dawn spread over the Eastern horizon and the fields of Texas spread out in every direction, I whispered an answer to the woman through the years.

"I'm so sorry. I don't know. I don't know when you let go."

I landed at Reagan National Airport in Washington and took the Metro train home. I set my laptop case on the wood floor of my small studio apartment and unpacked my piece of carry-on luggage. When everything was put away, I took my journal out of the laptop case and opened it up. I didn't open it to any written section—not to my dad's words, or to a particular day—but to the blank section I had not yet reached. I aimed for the pages that were split slightly farther apart, indicating the presence of a foreign object amid the journal's crisp pages and fragrant leather binding. The item it contained was suddenly visible like a pearl in an oyster.

It was an old photo of Michael—the one my brother took at the National Cemetery at the Presidio. I had kept it in my journals as they changed over the years—dozens of journals carried all over the United States. Even when I had felt far away from him, believed he didn't care, even when the necklace hit the trash bag, I had kept the photo. I pulled it out of the journal, sat on the bed, and looked at it. He was kneeling next to the grave of Pauline Fryer, the spy, holding the memorial wreath for the Union soldiers killed in the Civil War. The array of stargazer lilies in the center of the wreath looked spectacular.

The entire cemetery had been decorated for Memorial Day. There was an American flag in front of each gravestone. The picture was taken on a cloudy day, but the sun shone through enough that my dad was squinting through his glasses as he smiled for Mark and the camera. His blue ball cap was rigid and unbent in a distinctly nerdy and unself-conscious way, and his button-down shirt was tucked crisply into his well-worn jeans. He looked like a fit schoolteacher on a field trip, surrounded by gravestones, patriotism, and eucalyptus trees. I looked at the picture, gazing at details and remembering.

I stood up, shaking off the reverie, and put away the last of my clothes from the trip. I took a shower and dried my hair, scrubbing my curls vigorously with the towel as my body slowly registered the strain of the trip. Slowly, routinely, I got in my pajamas and lay down on my simple blue-checked rug. Suddenly I was vacant. Outside, DC pulsed with life. The apartment was calm and still. The motion and bustle of the capital swirled all around me.

Separate.

Apart.

I'll probably never see Dad again.

I lay there, like some kind of human jacket that God had tossed carelessly to the side, splayed out on the rug, feeling its coarse fibers against my arms and the firm flatness of the floor, and watched the ceiling fan slowly spinning, spinning, spinning.

Later that evening I decided to try to call him. I didn't expect to be able to talk with him; I was afraid I'd hear that he'd passed moments ago. I tried to scrunch myself up into a tight, impermeable ball in order to hear the news.

Beth answered.

"Oh, hi, Tiffany! Your dad is right here. Let me get him."

My heart lit up.

My dad's voice came through the receiver. He sounded stronger—so happy. He immediately bubbled over about the weekend.

"God puts things together in such extraordinary ways! I am just amazed! Seeing you and Mark . . . that's why I survived this past weekend. That's why I'm alive right now. When you both came in together, that was the best thing in my life."

At first I didn't believe him.

The best thing in his life? The best things in life are those you know really well, that are a part of your spirit. We weren't. . . .

Wait. Are we? Have I, all these years, been inadvertently breaking his heart?

"At noon, I didn't think I was going to live to see you together again. On many different levels I'm looking forward to dying, but when you walked in together on Saturday, you gave me more life than I ever had. You really helped me."

I remembered the way he looked when Mark and I entered the hospital room. He had been awaiting death like a gift. I saw it in his posture and the set of his jaw. He didn't want the pain anymore. I understood it. And then I recalled how he looked right before I left, the power and invigorated look in his eyes. He was a different man.

He spent time examining all of the improbable, amazing coincidences that aligned to help make our reunion possible. So much of our time growing up and visiting him was full of details and logistics, long hours figuring out vacation days and leave, packing family time into narrow weekend windows, deciding which parent had us for what holiday. It was all very much a hassle. But not this time.

I was already in Texas (a one percent chance, considering travel the last year, and I would not have been able to afford a last-minute flight); Mark got a flight quickly and was able to come; Anna had a car and offered to take me to San Antonio—unforgettable generosity. Everything worked out in the most perfect way to bring us all to the same place, aided by the heartfelt support of friends. The universe had to know, had to be behind it. We both agreed: Everything just aligned.

He observed how sometimes things just fit together like magic. Something that would normally be impossible was suddenly easy. We talked about signs—the tiny moments in life that point to greater meaning. Whether it involved noticing an object, catching sight of a newspaper headline, or a split second that just seemed suspended in eternity—you wonder why you even noticed it, and then suddenly, something dramatic happens that the small thing represented.

"I wonder if there's a name for that, Dad. You know, the signs. It seems like there should be. Déjà vu has a name. This is kind of like that."

"There is a name. Catholics call it a 'signal grace.' It's a sign that God's listening to you and directing you all the time. You see these moments by the grace of God. It indicates that you're on the right path and that God is helping and guiding you."

I grabbed a pen. I wanted to remember that and research it later. I wrote in large capital letters at the top of the page: *SIGNAL GRACE.*

My dad chuckled. "Man plans. God laughs. Tiffany, if this is the last time we talk, I'm really proud of you, and I pray for you every night."

Every night? I stared at the big letters and traced over them again. My hand trembled so much that, when I finished, the two words *signal grace* looked like they were vibrating. *He must mean recently.*

"My prayer time is kind of messed up because of the medication. Tonight I'll include Mom." He paused and then said, "I remember the first time I took you to Mardi Gras. After the parade, Grandma made a huge pan of meatballs. We just attacked those meatballs like we hadn't eaten! There was another time . . . two funny times. We were walking down St. Charles Avenue in New Orleans. It was during one of our trips. . . ."

I was immediately transported to New Orleans. Mardi Gras! Going to see the parades of the different krewes. Hats, crowds, and beads. Colorful floats that passed by, followed by huge marching bands and mounted riders in elaborate costumes. Smiling at Dad and Mark, smelling the strange, sweet stench of the gutters of New Orleans. Mardi Gras colors everywhere: purple, green, and gold. They had meanings, those colors. What were the meanings?

I tried to remember.

Purple was justice. Gold was power. And green? What was green?

The fantastic Louisiana marching bands made the earth and the city shake with thunderous rhythms of gaiety. I remembered being close to a young black high school boy as he passed by in the band. He was absorbed in playing the tuba, moving his body to the music like he carried no burden at all. The old streetlights and neon crowns of the revelers reflected off the brass of the tuba, off the shiny buttons on his uniform, and turned him into an accidental kaleidoscope of color. He didn't know, didn't care. The boy was lost in the moment. He was moving. He was music. The beat was pulsing through all things, and the crowd was following the band into ecstatic oblivion. He had turned himself into rhythm and life—and it was gorgeous.

Oh—faith. I remembered it now. Green was faith.

My dad continued. "It was eight or nine o'clock at night. There were you, me, and Mark walking down the street. You were in high school by then; you must've been about sixteen. All of a sudden . . . there's a military term called 'eyes right.' Well, you had to go to the bathroom and walked that way. All of these Tulane guys saw you and they did an 'eyes right'—it was like ten or twelve guys!" He chuckled again. "I think that was near Carrolton or Claiborne. And then the other time was at Burger King, on that same trip. There was a group of young ladies. You have such great posture and carry yourself so well. All of these girls did an 'eyes right.'

"So charming! All of these little girls looked at you. . . ."

I remembered the guys; I had tried to ignore them. I looked away and stared at who knows what while walking by—some trees, a streetlight, whatever—just something to get me past them. I didn't know why they were watching me. But I didn't recall seeing the girls.

"And then there was the day—Mom and I both agree, even after all these years, that it was the worst day of our lives. Tiffany, there are some people who say, 'I'm not sure if I have heard the voice of God in my life.' Well," he added with absolute conviction, "I have heard the voice of God."

HOLDING HANDS

"You were just a baby. I was putting you to bed. Mom was in the living room. I can't remember now. . . . I can't remember what she was doing. But I set you down in your crib and something told me: 'Don't leave her. Don't let her go. Don't walk out of this room.'"

I had heard this story before, but he told it with so much enthusiasm that I listened intently. It never got old.

"So I stayed. I stayed there and I watched you. And as I was watching you, your hands started to turn blue. Bright blue."

I imagined myself as him. How he felt. How I'd feel if it were my child.

"The color started to creep up your arm. I grabbed you, brought you into the living room, and told Mom we had to go to the hospital. She took one look at you and . . . oh . . ." His voice trailed off.

I wondered if he'd continue with the story, or talk about something else.

"She was shocked, horrified. It was awful. She grabbed the keys and we took you to the hospital. We were there for hours. They did several spinal taps on you. They couldn't get it right because you were so small. Mom and I agreed that if you didn't live we were never going to have another baby. You're the reason Mark is here. If we hadn't brought you to the hospital right then, the ER staff was convinced you would have been a SIDS death.

"God wanted you to live, Tiffany. God needed you to be in this life."

I looked down at the floor and supported my forehead with my hand. His words were beautiful, but I sat there unmoved. Life had been awfully dark and difficult lately; I didn't feel like a part of any plan at all. More like a misfit or a walking testament to the accidental and ridiculous.

All of my life I have connected with people by reveling in their joys whenever possible, but I tried to be judicious and authentic, to do so only when I found a corresponding truth within myself; when I could relax into, and not conjure, resonance. I didn't want to be the death of such a touching sentiment, but I felt nothing. I was the dampening pedal of a piano, silencing grand music, or the small metal cone snuffing out the candle's light. God absolutely did not need me in this life. It seemed like a denial of my father to not agree, though, so I implied support by remaining silent.

He talked, reminisced some more about the army, about being deployed to Bosnia. Searching again for connection, I strained to recall something we shared together. Anything we could talk about now. I remembered a picture he had sent me when he was overseas, and laughed.

"I still have that photograph that you took in Bosnia, Dad—the one with the Humvee and the sky that looks so beautiful. Remember it?" As I spoke, I got up and reached into a drawer. I found the photo in a tiny bag. I lay back down on my colorful comforter and looked at it as he spoke.

"Oh, my gosh, yes. That was one of the most amazing skies I've ever seen. I took that picture and didn't realize what I had until I got it developed later on. It was like heaven over hell."

As I looked at the lower third of the photo, at the parched and scorched earth, the rough Humvee, and the home in ruins, it did look like hell. But above the dark hues of the earth and the ruins of what men made, in the vast sky that humans could not build upon or blow up, there arched magnificent clouds, billowing and floating in spectacular display, as if moved by the hidden hand of the Almighty.

He paused, perhaps considering how to say what he wanted to say next. "Once you can get a spiritual focus, it enriches your life. I know how it's gonna end. It's gonna end on a happy note. I'll be so glad to get this pain over with. I don't want to put people through it. Whenever I die . . . if I die and you and Mark aren't here . . ."

I muted the phone and covered the receiver with my hand for good measure. I didn't want him to hear me cry.

"It's just the way God wants it. If you and Mark aren't here, don't feel bad. Don't feel like you let something go awry."

Too late.

"I'm really glad we did this. This has been a great conversation. I guess I'm getting a little tired and . . . I'm just so glad that we could take this journey together. Don't make any plans to fly down here until I hear from my surgeon on Friday. Have a good night tonight and sleep well and I love you bunches."

Get the words out. Steady voice.

"I love you too, Dad."

❧

I hung up the phone and sat still.

Journey.

I know he meant life when he said it, but I had never, when I was alone and quiet (which is when it matters), felt like we were together, or on the same team. I always felt as if I were by myself. Now I felt like someone who suddenly discovered they had a travel companion, a living person under their seat cushion: *You were with me all the time?* My mind suddenly bustled and skipped with excitement—*Boy, we could have had some fun together!* And then the joy departed as fast as it arrived: *The journey is ending.*

FREDERICKSBURG

The days passed slowly, each more likely "the one." I worked hard to extract meaning from the old, now empty routines of my life in DC. I went to the office, worked out regularly at the gym, and tried to eat well. But when all was said and done, I was just going through the motions. In the evenings, I called San Antonio and Beth offered updates. Michael would get on the line if he could, but sometimes it was short, and sometimes he did not. We would never again have another extended conversation. One day, as Beth and I talked on the phone, she said unexpectedly, "Tiff, do you remember that piñata you brought to your dad's hospital room?"

"Yes, of course." *How could I forget?* I had never felt as unsuccessful in life as I did when I couldn't offer him anything else finer—or more thoughtful— than a damn fiesta donkey made out of paper. It didn't even have any candy in it.

"You know, I meant to tell you later," Beth said, "and have been meaning to tell you for quite some time: That was really cheery. I didn't realize how dark and sad that hospital room was until you brought all of those colors in."

Really? "Well, thanks for saying that. I was afraid it was dorky, but it was all I could afford."

"No, no. It was very cool. And very thoughtful. Your dad and I both liked it. I just wanted to tell you."

The weeks passed and Memorial Day approached—one of Michael's favorite holidays: Christmas, New Year's, and Memorial Day.

I was not looking forward to it.

He had been on my mind constantly. Depression circled me like a hungry vulture. Something a little special and out of the ordinary might perk up my spirits. I needed to plan something. I didn't want to fly anywhere, though—not with all of the crowds in airports for holiday weekends. My friends were either traveling or hanging out with their families. I certainly didn't want to spend the holiday weekend alone in my dark studio apartment, growing self-destructive, stuck somewhere just thinking. Was there a more perfect hell?

I had sworn to myself when I first moved to Washington that I would make a diligent effort to visit the Civil War battlefields in the area, but I hadn't been to many. I had, in fact, been only to the battlefield in Fredericksburg, Virginia—and not for long. I decided to drive back to Fredericksburg and see more. My goal was just to survive the weekend without self-destructing or blowing my budget.

Fredericksburg is situated about fifty miles south of Washington, DC, almost exactly halfway between the District of Columbia (which was the capital of the Union) and Richmond, Virginia (the capital of the Confederacy). Predictably, the city was an epicenter of Civil War battles. Present-day residents routinely find old bullets in their backyards, and tales of ghosts and mysterious happenings swirl around the region.

That seemed good enough.

I left DC early on Saturday to avoid the traffic that turns I-95, the major north–south interstate that travels the length of the eastern seaboard between New York and Florida, into a frustrating parking lot. The fifty miles between Washington and Fredericksburg can take the unlucky traveler two and a half hours on a rough day. To avoid delays, I hit the highway at sunrise. Listening to music, I lost myself in reverie and watched the gorgeous countryside of the Piedmont region of Virginia pass by, glistening with dew in the morning sunshine.

When I arrived in the historic part of Fredericksburg, I meandered through the downtown shops and got some food at a nearby restaurant. Around noon, I wandered over to the battlefield. When I got there, dismay flooded me. Dozens of people were milling around. Parking in the adjacent neighborhood was hard to come by.

What is this? I grumbled inwardly. I wanted to go to a peaceful and quiet place; I didn't want to hang out around crowds. I didn't think the National Park Service, which managed the battlefield, would have anything going on for Memorial Day, but I should have known.

I managed to find a parking spot some distance away from the battlefield. I walked toward the old stone wall that, more than a century ago, was the center of the combat action, the ill-fated Union infantry charges against the entrenched Confederate position. As I approached, a friendly dad struck up a conversation. He talked to me, but looked distracted as he watched his son nearby.

"What's happening today?" I asked.

"Everyone is getting ready for the Luminaria," he replied. "It's an event to honor the soldiers who fell in the battle. The Union soldiers are all buried in that hillside cemetery on the old battlefield. Kids from the Fredericksburg region all go around and light the candles in the cemetery at sunset. It's pretty cool." He looked me square in the eye. "You should come back tonight and see it."

Sometimes God talks through people. Simple words resonate in a peculiar way and seem unusually important. The words rang in the back of my mind. *You should come back tonight and see it.* It sounded like guidance.

I shook my head clear. "Thanks," I said, "I will."

⌇

And so I found myself, hours later, in a quiet part of the cemetery at twilight, thinking about my dad and the spy. Candlelight flickered against nearby tombstones. The golden halos of light made the cold stones glow with attractive brilliance, making them warm and merry. The carved numbers on the headstones flashed in and out of clarity as the candlelight flickered and the summer breeze swept across the hill. It was not Fryer's grave, the spy, but it could have been. And here it was, Memorial Day weekend again—in another cemetery, next to another fallen soul who had fought for the unity of America, just like all those years ago with my dad in San Francisco on the other coast. The evening was so beautiful and the hundreds of lights so inspiring that for a moment I relaxed and forgot about being sad. I didn't understand life at all. I didn't know what I was doing. But that night, right at that moment, everything felt connected.

Lightning bugs flickered near the large trees of the cemetery several yards away. I looked down the aisle of graves—to the Girl Scouts and Boy Scouts rearranging some of the memorial lanterns. The entire row, the entire hillside, was a sprinkling of gorgeous lights. Although it had been crowded earlier in the day, the hillside was almost deserted now, except for the little kids scurrying around and giggling. I turned around, trying to step between the graves.

The cemetery was big. A lot of soldiers died in the Battle of Fredericksburg. It was a landmark battle, the location of a great Southern victory. I had never paid attention to it until I moved to the East Coast. Antietam and Gettysburg had always been the big battles in my mind, especially after reading *The Killer Angels* all those years ago. Fredericksburg was just one name among many in the history books.

I found out later that the Battle of Fredericksburg and its aftermath marked a difficult time for President Abraham Lincoln. Lincoln had dark moments—moments that tested his resolve and threw him, everything he believed and all of his efforts, into doubt. One of Lincoln's dark moments was immediately after Fredericksburg. Upon hearing of the Union's horrible, bloody defeat, facing a nation of people increasingly unhappy with his leadership, and trying to hold together the warring factions of an entire country, Lincoln wrote simply, *If there is a place worse than Hell, I am in it.*

I thought about the dead president, my dad, and my life as I sat on the hillside. As I looked into the deepening twilight over the roofs of Fredericksburg, sitting among the graves and the twinkling candles, I considered the lessons that could be learned and asked for the dead souls to please help me if they could—to do what, I didn't know.

I'm sorry. Please help me help the world, I guess. Please help me forgive myself for all the mistakes I've made.

I took a deep breath, focusing on the darkened horizon, and saw the first stars.

ONE LAST MESSAGE

My father was up at three a.m. one night shortly before he died. He wrote me a text. I loved the way he wrote texts. They were deliciously quaint. He wrote them in the same way most people write letters. He had a salutation (usually *Dear*, or *Hello*) and then the message, and always signed it. At first, I chalked it up to a generational thing and figured his texting style would change as he got used to sending them. I was wrong: It never changed. However, I loved his style so much that I changed mine. Ever since he wrote that text, I'd kept it on my phone. I had even thought about contacting the phone company to see if there was some way I could permanently save it. I didn't ever want to forget it, or lose it. I had just recently thanked him for some well wishes, and his response felt like his last and most important message.

His text, from the watches of the night, read:

Hello, Tiffany
You are very welcome! I just want you to know how much I love you and I will always love you and I am so very proud of you!

I always want the very best for you and wish God's blessings on you always. No matter how things might end for me just know that in the long run, I am OK in Heaven and things will be OK and that you are loved.

We just have to have Faith in God even though we don't know or understand His Ways.

Also please know that when your time and Mark's time draws close, don't be afraid, because Grandma and I will be close by waiting to bring you all back home to Heaven.

Love always, Dad

THE RETURN OF ST. ANTHONY

My father became emaciated. At almost six feet tall, he weighed only 108 pounds. In photos, he looked like a prisoner in a concentration camp. The cancer prevented his body from digesting food properly. His body had wasted away. It was impossible for him to sit comfortably, because there was no fat to cushion his frame. He moved slowly, gingerly. He had long ago stopped talking on the phone. Now, when I called, it was just Beth and updates on his decline. I came to understand how senior commanders might feel in a war they were losing: the dread of the briefing, the constant vigilance, the incomparable respect for the people on the front lines.

In the beginning of August, my dad took a turn for the worse. He was in a coma now, unconscious in a hospital bed, with the doctors wondering how he had lived so long already. They had told him, when he went in for surgery, that he had about two days to live; it had been five months. He was always at the back of my mind. The backdrop for my days was hushed and resigned loneliness.

One evening I returned home, unlatched the front door, and immediately knew something was wrong. But try as I might, I couldn't pinpoint the feeling. *What is wrong with this picture?*

Suddenly, I realized my right hand felt odd somehow: empty and light. I looked down and saw, where my Texas A&M ring usually nestled on my ring finger, that there was nothing but a small tan line. *Oh, no!* I had a sinking feeling and knew the truth before I even tried to find the ring. Even so, I looked all over the studio and tried to think of every place I had been that day. It was gone! The ring he told me to buy. The ring I had worn almost every day since graduating. I had lost weight and the ring had become wiggly where it once sat snug. It probably just slipped off my finger.

I went to the gym but could not find the ring. Nobody had seen it.

Feeling like everything meaningful was slowly disappearing, I returned to my studio in DC. I entered my apartment, locked the front door as usual, and took a couple of strides into the small space that served as both the living room and bedroom. I crumpled to the floor in fatigue—my last few workouts had been hard, and worry was taking its toll. I leaned against the striped comforter of the bed. The simple wooden bed frame creaked with my weight. A good friend had once told me that the best way to find something was to let go of it. I did not quite know what that meant, but I could tell something within me was stuck—and stuck hard—on that ring.

I closed my eyes and tried to clear my thoughts of the ring and all that it meant to me. I tried to disengage it from all of the happier memories of college: my few great friends, the warm days on the beach, and the quiet feeling of achievement when I got the ring. No one could know how hard slogging through college was for me, from the lonely nights to trying so hard to be positive and uplifting for other people—when I felt empty and dark myself. I remembered my dad's strength through all those years, and the moment on the porch at the little beach house when he stood there saying good-bye. Suddenly I realized what it was I had sensed that day. I paused, frozen in the memory.

He loves me.

He didn't give me a home during high school or help me during college out of obligation or responsibility. I never knew. I never really understood

Why didn't I see? Why didn't I understand? He really and truly loves me.

After a long moment, communing with that realization, something within me released its desperate death grip on the ring. I consciously let go of it.

In the space of peace that immediately followed, a soft plume of thought rose in the sky of my mind: *The ring is a lost thing.*

Saint Anthony.

Saint Anthony can find a lost thing.

Something about Saint Anthony felt like an old friend and always had. I never understood why, but I had felt it ever since my dad first told me about him all those years ago. Maybe the comforting feeling was stronger because of all of the good memories in the city named for him. Maybe it was something else. The ring itself was no longer important, but with a sudden sense of purpose I flipped over on the carpet so I was facing the bed and knelt like a child. I prayed.

"Dear Saint Anthony, I know I don't talk to you enough, and I'm sorry about that. I lost my college ring—I am sure you already know that—and I would really like it back. If I can't have it, or if it isn't meant to be, that's okay; please help me to continue to let go of it. But if I could have it back, that would be great."

I paused and let myself be very quiet. The next words surfaced naturally and sincerely from my heart: "Thank you. I love you. Amen."

I went to sleep with calmer thoughts, hoping my dad was having a good night.

❧

A few days later, I went into the gym for my daily workout. Routine had become a lifeline. As I headed for the women's locker room, the desk attendant, a tall young man with a ready smile, exclaimed, "Oh, wait! I think I have something for you. . . ." He reached underneath the desk. "Your last name is Yates, right?"

"Yep, that's me."

"Okay, yeah. Here you go." He handed me a simple, slightly crinkled white envelope. My last name was written in large, bold strokes in a Sharpie marker on the front.

I reached out and took it. Nestled inside the crumpled white paper was my Texas A&M class ring. I blinked and looked up from under my ball cap in surprise.

"I-I really didn't think I would ever see this again. Where did you find it?" I was elated. Suddenly, it seemed like maybe someone upstairs was actually listening.

"I didn't. One of the other staff found it in the ladies' locker room."

"Well, thank you! Thank you very much!"

He nodded and smiled.

I put the ring on. As I headed to the locker room, I whispered, "Thank you."

THE HAWK

On the morning of August 10, 2010, I went to work as usual. I got to my office on the seventh floor, set my stuff down in my cubicle, and went to talk to my coworker Tina. Tina was a ball of energy and humor, with the ability to fearlessly say anything to anyone. I went into her office almost as if going to a gas station, to fuel up on someone else's positivity and strength. I leaned against the doorframe as we chatted.

Tina complained, "I've been trying to age like a fine wine, but it's ending up more like a shot of whiskey and a stale cigarette."

I laughed. All of a sudden, a movement in the window behind her shoulder caught my eye. A great red bird was perched on the building ledge outside the office.

"Oh, my God! Is that a hawk?" I exclaimed.

Tina twisted quickly in her chair.

"Whoa! Yes!" she blurted. "Holy cow, I've never seen one of those here!"

We rushed from her office to my area around the corner to get a better angle. The hawk was still there. Tina and I took pictures and wondered idly what species it was. We had both seen crows on the ledge before, but never a large bird of prey.

"If only there were somebody around here who knew something about hawks," I said.

"Yeah, it would be nice to know!"

As she positioned for another photo, a computer technician appeared down the hall. It was Wendy, a blond, bubbly woman who fixed everything that our staff broke, and ministered to the gremlins within our software. She walked hastily—her normal workday pace—and greeted us with a genuine grin.

"Hey, guys!"

"Look!" We both pointed to the hawk outside.

Wendy glanced curiously toward the window. Her eyes lit up. "Oh, my gosh! That's a red-tailed hawk!"

I looked at her in surprise. "How do you know that?"

"I used to work at a wild bird center," she said. I gave Tina an astonished, *well, how about that* look. Wendy eagerly shared facts about the birds, amazed that one would be hanging out on the seventh floor of an office building near DC.

She said, "It's big, even for a red-tailed hawk."

The hawk's power and presence were magnificent, and made everything in the office seem drab and pedestrian. It remained balanced on the corner of the large patio area, as still as a statue, surveying the entire boulevard. It looked, perched so, like the ruler of a kingdom, and had a sinuous, lightning-fast way of moving its head atop the breathless stillness of its body that made me realize the powerful nature behind the simple word *hunter*. We continued to watch, discussing everything about it—its coloring, body, and feathers—until, at almost exactly nine a.m., in a single, suspended motion, it spread its great wings and soared out of sight.

◦❦◦

A couple hours later, my phone lit up with an incoming call. It was from Beth. My heart sank. I walked quietly into the deputy director's vacant office for a moment of privacy and answered the phone.

There was a telltale pause and a ragged, shaky breath. Beth was crying.

Oh, no.

"Tiffany, I'm sorry to call you at work, but I just wanted you to know . . . your dad died this morning."

I looked out of the windows of the beautiful corner office, over the trees and buildings of southern Maryland, and suddenly felt as if San Antonio were galaxies away, as if Beth were calling me from a different dimension. My mind, after a moment of frozen absolute silence, was suddenly clear and childlike, connecting things in peculiar ways, trying to align itself, to adjust. I had been expecting the words, but when I heard them, I experienced nothing but pure confusion: *What does that mean?*

Your dad died this morning.

He did, did he? I wonder how that felt.

Did you talk with him afterward?

Abruptly, bizarrely, it seemed as if I ought to be hearing from him soon, as though he'd be showing up on my doorstep in a few hours, having taken a flight to DC. And then, a moment of clarity: *No. You can't talk to him. He's not here anymore.*

"He passed away around eight a.m. It would have been nine a.m. your time." Beth gasped, having trouble breathing through the tears. "I'm so sorry. He was such a strong man, and his spirit . . . I know his spirit was the only thing that made him live so long."

My mind now crashed about in a tumult. *He died. Dying is when people don't come back. That's when you can never speak to them again.*

Suddenly, unexpectedly, something strong within me spoke up ferociously. Everything else was silent again for a moment. The strong voice pronounced judgment.

He has a heart, and hearts don't just die. They live forever.

I did not feel grief, just shock. Aside from my mind's furious efforts, I felt empty. I didn't feel anything that I expected. In fact, the only thing I knew I wanted was to make Beth understand how much I appreciated—really appreciated—her calling to tell me the news. I wanted to comfort her.

"Beth, thank you . . . Thank you so much for calling me. I can't talk a lot now, but I'll call you later today. I love you and will talk to you soon."

She said gently, sweetly, "Okay, love you too. I'll talk to you soon." Her voice sounded calmer.

I hung up the phone and inhaled. I opened the office door, almost colliding with my boss, Debra. Tina was right beside her. They had obviously been immersed in an intense discussion about work, heading into Debra's office, which was right beside the one I was in. Both of them reacted in such a way that I realized my face must reveal more than I thought. I nodded to them but kept walking. *I need to get out for a while and focus.* I grabbed my keys and wallet as I passed my desk.

From behind me, Tina asked what I thought was an inordinately random question: "Will you be back?"

I managed three clipped words: "Yes. I will."

As I left the building and walked through the sunshine to my car, absorbed in my thoughts, I remembered the hawk.

Flying away.

. . . would have been nine a.m. your time . . .

Nine a.m.

I got in my car and left the small campus of buildings and offices. I wanted a little corner of life where I could just retreat for a moment and not be surprised by someone bumbling into my space. I didn't want the demands of others. And I realized I needed to call my mom to tell her the news. I parked the car near a small French restaurant called La Madeleine and just sat in the driver's seat, staring for a moment out the window, visualizing where my mom might be and how she might take the news.

I dialed her number, and when she answered, I gathered from her reaction that she knew what I was calling about even before she even picked up the phone. She was supportive, kind, but I didn't need it.

When I returned to the office, word had clearly spread that something had happened in my world. My coworkers gave me plenty of space and spoke in softer tones than normal. I took a moment to tell Debra what had happened.

She leaned forward, composed and comforting. "If you need to leave, go ahead and leave. Everything will be okay."

"I would like, if it's okay with you, to stay for a while today," I replied. "It would help me to stay."

Debra nodded. "Of course. Please let me know if there's anything I can do to help."

Tina stopped by my desk later that afternoon—a deliberate visit. She called me by her pet name for me: "Tiffy, I know this isn't an easy day. I lost my dad and I'm still a mess about it sometimes . . . you know that. But I've been around a long time, and I know a sign when I see it. That hawk—that was a sign from your dad. I've seen a lot of signs, but that one . . . that one just gives me shivers. So know it. Know that that hawk was your dad saying good-bye."

She looked intently at me and said, "It was beautiful."

I remembered the hawk. I saw it flying away again—she was right. As she walked away, I put my elbow on the table, resting my head in my hand, and gazed at the wood grain of my desk. The hawk was so inspiring. If that was the essence of his spirit, I wish I had seen that power and that beauty before today.

OF HALVES AND WHOLES

The next day, Tina came into the office and handed me an envelope. She said, "It's heavy stuff. You might want to wait until after work to read it."

I raised my eyebrows and regarded her. Tina was hilarious and inane when skies were clear, but if things got cloudy, she wasn't one for drama. I took her advice and waited. When I got home after work, I split the seal and opened the envelope. A check for a thousand dollars fell out.

My eyes popped open. In the accompanying letter, she wrote at length of her own grief when her father passed away, and how she wanted to make sure I had enough money to fly out for my dad's funeral if I wanted to go. I felt so touched that someone would be so generous with their own wealth, to help at such a time, that I stared for several minutes into space, alone in my apartment, wondering at the unsung glory of good people.

There was no funeral planned. Michael's body was to be cremated and the ashes spread near the Lookout Point in the Presidio that he loved so much. He had specifically requested that.

As I sat, I resolved to give something back to my friend, even though I had no intention of cashing the check. It was such a beautiful, bighearted gesture that I wanted to say thank-you in a meaningful way. I started to think of things I could do. Things I could give. Suddenly, I remembered Kahlil Gibran's great book *The Prophet*, and his insight about giving and gifts. He wrote about how bad it is—destructive, even—to feel too indebted to someone who has given you a present. In lilting language and touching imagery, he spoke of how both the recipient and the giver get dragged down by a sense of obligation. Encouraging everybody to allow true generosity to lift them up, he asserted that people need to allow goodness and grace to bless them, to have faith in the kindness of their fellow man, because every person is nothing less than a child of God the Father.

That's right, I thought. *Sometimes I forget.*
God the Father.
I felt freer, remembering that. I would say thank-you and mean it. She would understand.

Immediately after my dad died, and for about a week, I had amazing dreams full of tenderness and contentment. My entire family was together and having fun. Everyone smiled and laughed; people hugged and sat close to one another. It was so real that I knew somehow it was true in spirit. They were all of the very moments that I wanted so much when I was young. I woke feeling happy every morning, like the best things in life—all of the things I had hoped were true— not only were true, but were the only *real* things. As the weeks wore on, the beautiful dreams slowly dissipated into normal dreams, infused occasionally with concerns and separations. Around that time, I started to wear the "Best Friends" half-circle necklace to work.

One morning, a coworker walked up to my desk and exclaimed, "Oh, you have a *mizpah!*"

"A what?" I looked at her, perplexed. *Was that English?*

"Your necklace. It's called a *mizpah*—it's jewelry that has two halves. It's supposed to be a symbol of people who have an inseparable bond. The actual word means something too. I can't remember the details, though. Check it out online! That's cool that you have one. I haven't seen one since high school."

I did some research. The word was from a line in the Bible (Genesis 31:49), which reads in the King James Version:

And Mizpah; for he said,
The LORD watch between me and thee,
when we are absent one from another.

Mizpah jewelry is often worn by loved ones who cannot be together, as a token of their affection and connection. It symbolizes both the separation of loved ones and the abiding presence and protection of God.

My eyebrows got higher and higher as I read. *Wow, if that's not a message, I don't know what is.* I found the coworker down the hall later that afternoon.

"Hey, I just wanted to tell you thank-you. I didn't know any of that about my necklace."

"You're welcome! I thought it was cool that you had one."

❧

Fall turned into winter and the barren trees covered the landscape. Two days after Christmas, I woke up and felt no enthusiasm for going to work. Nothing in my heart wanted what the day promised. There was no excitement about projects or people. I went through the motions of getting dressed for another day in the office, empty within myself. Hardly anyone was going to be there anyway—it was the week between Christmas and New Year's, for crying out loud. I had family, but no one lived close by, and at this late date a flight somewhere would cost a fortune. I didn't have a whole lot of leave left, and hadn't planned on a large holiday trip. My friends were either out of town or working. It felt to me as though someone had plopped me into the world, giving me the trappings of life but none of the meaning.

I ached to leave and go somewhere. I could get excited about packing up my car and hitting the road. I had never been to several of the big tourist attractions nearby: Harper's Ferry, Virginia Beach, or Lancaster. Or even Gettysburg, Pennsylvania.

All those years ago I couldn't wait to go to Gettysburg. I remembered Michael's curiosity about anything and everything; the way he dove into life and knowledge like he couldn't get enough of it. The way he wasn't afraid of what other people thought; how he did his own thing. I recalled some of my favorite parts of *The Killer Angels*, and watching the movie *Gettysburg* later with both my mom and Mark. *That might be a really cool visit!* A celebration of all of us—and the history we enjoyed together. It was only a couple of hours away and I hadn't gone yet. I decided I'd go this weekend.

I opted to pack a small overnight bag, just in case. I could leave straight from work. I went to the office as usual, but as soon as I got to my desk, I knew I couldn't stay. My heart wasn't there. There was no forcing it today.

I told Tina and Laura how I was feeling. Tina pointed out that this was the first Christmas since my dad had died, and maybe that was why I was sad. *It could be*, I thought.

I left the office within a half hour of entering it. I didn't have enough energy to sacrifice for work today. I didn't even have enough for myself. When the engine of my little Nissan Sentra revved up in the parking lot, though, I felt like a giant weight had been lifted. I headed north, deeper into Maryland—past the urban sprawl of Rockville and Gaithersburg, and then farther into Germantown. The houses started dwindling and the countryside ascending; the hills, now stripped of humanity's sprawling commercial presence, presided over farms and modest highways in natural grandeur.

Why do I live in the city? I asked myself. *Maryland is so beautiful!* The scenery glided by as the little black car hummed on. Frederick, Maryland, made a highway cameo, appearing and disappearing just as quickly. When I saw the sign for Pennsylvania, I felt lighter and free. The license plates changed colors. Drivers were slower and more mellow.

The state line between Maryland and Pennsylvania is like crossing the border between countries, the two states are so vastly different. It's not just a simple state border: It's the Mason-Dixon Line, a boundary methodically surveyed to end a bloody argument over property between the colonies of Maryland and Pennsylvania. However, the line became the symbolic boundary between the North and South in the Civil War. "Dixie," the nickname for the South, comes from a variation of "Mason-Dixon." Crown stones, large boulders that were used to mark the border every five miles as the surveyors moved across the land, are still visible along parts of it.

I headed into the heart of the North. The Union.

As I approached Gettysburg, I did not have a good idea of where to turn, and hoped that some signs would lead the way to the battlefield. I remembered some road names from the story about the battle—Taneytown, Emmitsburg, and Chambersburg—but they were nothing but pocket lint in my mind. I had no context for them, and trying to create a mental map of the city was futile.

As I approached Gettysburg, I began to see signs for the battlefield itself. A few more turns and I found a ranger station. There were no cars on the road here. I braved the cold to go in and pick up a park map with the battlefield highlights. I wanted to see the land over which the Confederates, in the climax of *The Killer Angels*, famously charged on the final day of the battle. That field was a little distance away. The closest point that really interested me was a hill called Little Round Top. The park ranger advised me to park at the bottom of the hill and hike to the top, mentioning that the only access road to the peak was one-way in the other direction. I thanked the park ranger and, slipping a bit on the icy sidewalk, trudged back to my car.

It's an adventurer's day, I thought as I started the engine. *It's beautiful . . . but in a cold and windy way.* I glanced at the map, got an idea of where I was. Little Round Top was about ten blocks and one right turn away. Old hospitals and battle markers lined the route. Within a couple minutes, I found the tiny parking lot that the park ranger recommended at the base of the hill.

I got out of my car and started up the lonely hill by myself. My boots crunched the frozen leaves and the wind gusted hard and fast. This place—so hot and tranquil in summer—was an icy wasteland. I huddled up. My sweater wasn't enough for the cold. It was oversize—one of Carter's that, as it turned out, I borrowed permanently (he would say "stole"). It let the chill in by bunching and crimping in its own mass, the folds of thick fabric creating tunnels of cold air against my skin. But I liked the sweater, and, feeling somewhat miserable already, I was also willing to feel cold. *Bring it on*, I thought. Something about the cold felt right. I'd rather be out among the bare trees on this afternoon than in the office or by a roaring fireplace. I walked on alone.

The hill was deserted and, for being so famous, did not look that big. From far away, in fact, it was hardly distinguishable from the gentle slopes that defined that part of Pennsylvania. I'd wondered before and wondered then whether perhaps I was missing a great and obvious fact about the hill. Then it occurred to me that my eyes were accustomed to and noticed different things from the eyes of a foot soldier in the 1860s. I watched for freeway signs, addresses, and store names. An infantryman wouldn't. *Now, what on earth would an infantryman—tired, walking, and carrying a canteen, gun, and ammunition—what would he notice? You've been on long hikes, Tiffany,* I told myself. *Why is this place different from the rest of the battlefield?*

I didn't see the difference then so much as feel it in my body. My heart rate climbed; my lungs expanded with desperation. I saw the gentle slope that suddenly made one breathe harder in the ascent. I aimed for the partially obscured monuments at the peak. *Must be where the action was.* I thought about my dad. I ached, but knew there wasn't a salve for this pain. I thought of kinder words I could have said and written; deeply wished I had demonstrated more patience and gratitude. I thought of the gifts, words, and efforts I had taken for granted or, in some cases, completely overlooked: his helping me put those little pennies into the loafers for school, teaching me how to write checks at the kitchen table, and making all of those trips to Galveston to see me while I was in college—trips that, for him, were two hours out of the way on an already long journey.

All this time I had been climbing steadily among the bare trees. I saw the surrounding countryside reveal itself like a book as I got higher and higher—first a page, then a chapter, then the entire story; the scenery lay out in front of me, the height of the hill obvious now. A blast of wind greeted me at the peak. I peered, for the first time, over the land on which the Confederates had advanced.

They tried to climb this?

I stood, dumbstruck. My path up the eastern side per the park ranger's advice had disguised the worst of the hill. The other face was rocky and steep, uninviting even under pleasant conditions. Bullets certainly wouldn't make it easier. I knew, from reading excerpts about the battle years ago, that the Confederates eventually moved and attacked the far left flank of the Union line to the south, but they had first tried this very spot. I surveyed the terrain, openmouthed, and turned toward history.

I went down the rocky side a short distance just to see what the view was like coming up. Again, I was amazed. *It looks almost safe!* When ascending, the rocks appeared to be a sheltering element—at least to my untrained eye—large boulders that offered solid, if temporary homes for the assailants. However, from above, they were the exact opposite. The rocks created pockets of clarity for the defenders, the stones framing empty spaces that would be filled with the vulnerable, mortal bodies of the enemies; their next step was obvious, inevitable.

I hiked back to the peak, grasping and slipping on massive boulders. I could see the entire dip in the earth to Devil's Den, a patch of low land and alien-looking rocks to the south. I imagined looking out over that land as men fought and fell, wounded or dying. The slant of the hill, from the top behind me to the jumbled mess of rocks nestled in the lower land, had the look and feel of an empty stage, as if the main actors had left—and now there wasn't even an audience. I took a breath and let the peace of a century flood me, the peace of men's spirits after they have left the earth. It was a quiet peace that couldn't be felt in a tour group, or even with another person. It was the reason I liked battlefields: to ask for comfort from others who had suffered; to go and just be in their presence. There are angels on battlefields.

I looked over a few of the hill's uppermost monuments and moved on. The wind in the open chilled me through to the bone.

I shivered. I moved down the hill to get warmer and to see the position of a famous Union regiment, the 20th Maine. Instead of giving up and retreating when the entire regiment ran out of ammunition, the commander ordered a bayonet charge. In doing so, the 20th Maine saved the Union Army on that side. As desperate as the defensive stand was, peace pervaded the area now.

Thinking of my dad, I headed back to the car. By the time I finally made it to the small parking lot, I was so cold that I could not move my fingers properly. I fumbled and swore under my breath, trying to function in the simplest task. I finally got in and sat rigidly—body shivering and teeth chattering—until the pain of heat came back into my fingers. Nausea and hunger gnawed at me.

I turned the car on, changed gears, and pulled out of the desolate parking lot onto the one-way street. I did not know where I was going, and knew only that I felt sick from lack of food. Loneliness wrenched at my gut. I regretted so much, convinced that Michael and I could have had happier moments, that our relationship would have been more pleasant and smooth if I had just done things differently somewhere along the line. But I couldn't identify the critical junctures, the moments I went wrong. Small, unrecognized errors had accumulated, like snowflakes, into an avalanche. I had tried to do my best, but I could have been more grateful, could have been more direct and honest. The frustration and negative thinking reached a crux: *Why am I even alive?*

I drove on, toward the central action of the last day, toward the culmination of the battle.

Despite the sadness and hunger, I slowed down and stopped occasionally to read the plaques on the battlefield monuments more closely. After all, it was not every day that I had the time to wander around the fields of Gettysburg. I started to read a large memorial and then stopped. My heart jumped into my throat in shock. It took a moment for my brain to process the stone, the chiseled shape that loomed above me.

No way, I thought. I took a step back.

The imposing monument in front of me, whose tiny engraving I stooped to read, held high on the battlefield the unmistakable form of an enormous shamrock.

Why is there a shamrock on a battlefield monument?

Then my knees went weak.

As I looked around, I realized I stood in the middle of the battlefield, and everywhere—all around me—were shamrocks. All of the monuments and memorials, each one solitary and quiet, were covered in three-leafed clovers of all sizes. Every variation of shamrocks imaginable could be seen from where I stood: large and small, some carved inches deep into solid granite, painstakingly engraved, and others jutting out from hard marble walls in bas-relief. I stood all alone in a field, a most unlikely place to be found during a holiday week, with one common symbol on everything nearby in all directions. Something welled up. From all around me rose a feeling of pervasive love, gently expanding like a tide of comfort on lonely shores. I knew right then.

He was there.

Dad.

The grey sky still reigned above, but there was sun and warmth from everywhere now. I stood stock-still and looked around at all of the different shamrocks.

Dad! Oh, my God! Thank you for loving me. Thank you showing me that you're around. I love you so much. More than I ever knew. Thank you for understanding and forgiving me.

I gazed once again at all of the shamrocks and then closed my eyes. Tears trickled down my cheeks. I stood alone on the battlefield, and yet sensed my dad all around. So much love. I took a deep breath. I let the air flood my lungs, felt the life in my body, and reached for the consciousness of my dad. A gentleness, a greatness so expansive and immaculate, was right there.

And moreover, it was very, very amused.

I grinned. *Yes. You got me, Dad.*

God, thank you for guiding me to the park ranger. Thank you for showing me to Little Round Top. Thank you for helping me to come this way. Who spends the holidays wandering a Civil War battlefield alone?

Suddenly the single day, narrowed down even to that very moment, and all of the many years expanding behind me like rising dust from the road of love—all fell into place. As disconnected and rootless as my life had seemed, events now all fit together perfectly. Flawlessly.

From seeing *The Killer Angels* on his bookshelf all those years ago and getting interested in the Civil War to the year at Incarnate Word with him in San Antonio. Even the violence and difficulties—between me and Fox, between my dad and my mom. The experiences were painful, even killing hopeful parts of us, but look where it brought us all now: to deeper understanding. I made mistakes, yes. We all did. But now I did know how to love people better.

Amid the growing quiet of my mind, my heart burst forth into my own consciousness. As if I were in deep meditation, I felt a rush of pure power within—my heart as it truly is, in a blessed and glorious moment—and saw that I had always known and loved my dad somehow, that years of pain and hurt had obscured the truth, but not changed it. Here was the feeling and truth in full glory. In pure, undiluted honesty. Arrestingly suspended in the sudden, unfamiliar beauty of my own heart, I was flooded, over and through, by gratitude and forgiveness; they rinsed away the grime of mistakes and judgment like a baptism, and made me feel radiant in glowing peace. Words came out—the merest distant fireworks of a joyful explosion from somewhere close to the heart of God: "I love you! Thank you."

THE GARDEN OF THE DEAD

I opened my eyes. I wiped the tears from my cheeks and started to walk, slowly, among the monuments. I had no direction in mind and no destination to reach. I walked as though the battleground were an elaborate garden, aware not only of the irony, but also somehow of the harmony of it all. The Japanese word for garden, *niwa*, means "pure place." It is a place purified for the worship of the gods. This place turned my heart to God. In that sense it was a magnificent garden—far more so than an array of colorful flowers. Something—my dad, the men who made the monuments, the men who died here—something turned this rough patch of earth, adorned as simply but sincerely as ever man achieved, into a place of awe and gratitude.

I decided to move a little farther down the field, toward the town of Gettysburg itself. I felt as if I were exploring with my dad right beside me. Like we were taking a walk together—as we used to when we were discovering some new place. I walked toward the larger monuments on the field. Out of the corner of my eye, a modest memorial in the form of a scroll caught my attention. Curiosity urged me on, despite the chill.

I'll go in a moment, I thought. *But first I want to see this one.*

I walked over to the monument. It was a Confederate one. I leaned in as close as I could. There was an officer's name on it: General Lewis Armistead. Hancock's friend! So this was where he was . . . or at least in the vicinity of this spot. Hancock would have walked and ridden all around this ground. He and Armistead fought directly against each other on this very field. I had completely forgotten about it. Armistead famously led his Confederate brigade in a successful—if temporary—breach of Hancock's Union line on the last day right here. Confirmed by many different accounts, Armistead pierced his own hat with his saber and held it aloft to inspire his brigade as he advanced. Wounded here, in front of the colors of his friend's army, he was—to hear the historians tell it—never able to speak to his friend again. He died in Gettysburg. Hancock, on the other hand, went on to run for president of the United States.

And that prayer book!

Armistead had given the Hancock family a prayer book.

Trust in God and fear nothing.

I looked around with eagerness, wondering whether some particular place would pop out in my mind as the actual spot on which Armistead, the great friend, fell on the battlefield. I wanted to kneel down on the same ground, as if doing so could help me tune in to that kind of courage, that kind of hero.

Nothing arose in my mind. No light on the field. No ghost arose in uniform to greet me. But I felt a sense of peace. I felt like I had done what I came here to do. I turned from the stone scroll and walked purposefully back to the car. *Thank you, Dad. Thank you for this day . . . and the comfort. Thank you.* I started the car and pulled onto the main asphalt trail across Cemetery Ridge. I was lost in thought as I came to the end of the park road, near the edge of the town. There was one last monument on my right before I turned onto the main modern road into town.

It was a giant, carved shamrock.

HEADED HOME

Ileft the battlefield feeling renewed. I grabbed a small snack in town; none of the sit-down restaurants looked appealing and affordable. I wished one had—a cozy atmosphere and some hearty food would have hit the spot. I headed back to DC, reminiscing about the day's astonishing coincidences. The afternoon waned and the sky slowly darkened as I took the on-ramp for Highway 15 back to Frederick, lost in thought. I drove the peaceful miles in a happy daze. A few miles down the road, I caught sight of a billboard.

Up ahead was a place called the Shamrock Restaurant.

Doubt and a fear of believing crept into my heart. Were these all just elaborate coincidences? Well, even if they were, I was going to eat there. The day had been too weird not to stop.

I drove on a few more miles until the roadside restaurant came into view. The large parking lot was half-full; it was not quite time for any dinner rush.

I went inside and was immediately, completely delighted. It was the perfect restaurant for the day! The dining room, partitioned into intimate sections, was dimly lit, warm and cozy, and decorated tastefully with tiny three-leafed clovers everywhere. A kind server sat me at a prime table even though I was alone, and left to get a menu and water.

The menu arrived, but I just asked the server what she suggested. She replied thoughtfully and honestly, and I ordered what she recommended. It wasn't the most expensive thing on the menu, and I appreciated that the woman took time to really consider her answer. The food was spectacular—hearty Irish fare with large servings. Again, I felt my dad's presence.

Everything I was wanting, and shamrocks everywhere, I thought. *What an amazing day.*

As I sat, my body relaxed. A tension that I did not even know I had been carrying around was dissipating into the air like steam. My belly felt content and my shoulders loosened, released from an unknown burden. My breathing came easier, and I suddenly felt more at ease than I normally did. I leaned back in the strong, solid chair, and breathed deeply.

This is so good.

I took my journal out and scribbled while the server refilled my water glass several times. I enjoyed every moment and tipped the server extra. As I was leaving, feeling renewed and immensely content, I passed the hostess station by the front door. Something flashed and sparkled on the dark wall. I leaned in for a closer look. It was a sculpted green shamrock with a gold engraving that caught the light and twinkled. A shamrock in that restaurant was not particularly unique, but the face of this one glittered with a single word: *Father.*

I stood there in shock.

I looked around to see whether there were any other engraved shamrocks like it. *It must be part of a set. Where's the Mother, Brother, or Aunt one? Or if it's religious maybe a Son or Holy Spirit one?* I actually thought I might feel more comfortable if there were another one.

But there was nothing. Not one. It was the only engraved shamrock.

I saw my server across the dining hall and gestured toward the wall. She came over and looked where I was pointing.

"Um," I stammered, "can I buy this shamrock? The one that says 'Father'?"

"I think so," she replied. "Let me check."

She left and returned, smiling; the manager had said sure.

I bought the small ornament and headed outside. The air was bitterly cold and the wind was blowing briskly. The restaurant had filled up; every parking spot was taken. As I got into my little black car, I set the small gift bag down on the passenger seat. I pulled the shamrock out of its bag and turned it over in my hand in the last light of day. Tears threatened to come. I started the car. Turning the radio on, I pulled out of the parking lot and onto the highway, singing along. And from behind, within, and all around me soared a sense of freedom and adventure, just like in the old days when it was my dad driving—on different highways—in another place and time.

HARMONY

When I got home, I researched the Battle of Gettysburg. It turned out that there was a good reason for shamrocks to be scattered all over Gettysburg. In the summer of 1863, the shamrock was the symbol of General Winfield Scott Hancock's Second Corps. The Second Corps' standard was a stylized trefoil. The word "trefoil" is a synonym for shamrock, from the Latin word *trifolium*, which simply means "three-leaved plant." It was considered by some to be symbolic of the Irish, who comprised a good deal of the Second Corps (including the famous Irish Brigade), and by others to be symbolic of God.

I returned to the office the following Monday. Well into the morning, Laura asked me about the trip to Gettysburg. I grinned and said, "It was pretty cool!"

I told her all about the chilly weather and wandering around the battlefield feeling lost and sad. Then I told her the rest of the story.

"Laura, there were hundreds of shamrocks. Literally. And not only that, but shamrocks appeared in a big way three times that day. You know the thing about threes? If something happens three times, then it's a real sign. There was the battlefield, the restaurant, and then the 'Father' ornament. . . ."

Laura shone with amazement. "Oh, my gosh, Tiffany! I want to see the shamrock. Bring it in sometime!"

Later that week, I brought in the small ornament. It had a luster that, when set against the backdrop of the supplies and furniture of the agency's offices, made everything else look bland and dingy. During the day, my boss, Debra, expressed some curiosity about it. I have always felt a little awkward answering personal inquiries—worried that others might think what was special to me was meaningless or unimportant. Especially at work, I felt a deep obligation to be efficient and remain a little aloof. Tina and Laura were exceptions to the rule—I joked with them all of the time. Debra, though, while I occasionally bantered with her, was still my boss—an accomplished executive working for the United States government. However, I admired her deeply, both professionally and personally. She had, over the course of the years I worked in the division, always conducted herself with professionalism and integrity, displaying thoughtful kindness to colleagues in moments that sparkled with genuine care. So I shared the entire story behind the ornament: my dad's choice of symbol, my sadness after his death, and the experience visiting Gettysburg. She listened and, as I finished, regarded the ornament again—this time in a different way. Then she looked at me and her keen blue eyes shone with friendliness and affection.

❧

When Mark, Beth, and I scattered Michael's ashes at the Presidio the following year, my hand curled, shockingly, around a small curved fragment of bone as I grabbed a handful. Involuntarily, I shuddered. I forced myself to keep a grip. *This was his body!* I wondered what body part it was, how long it served him, and how, looking at him years ago, I'd never have guessed that one day I'd be holding this bone.

Together, we looked at one another to synchronize the toss to God as we stood among the briars and trees of the weathered hillside. We tossed the ashes simultaneously into the fragrant breeze; the moment we did, surprise flooded me. The ashes went up, up into the air, carried on the wind over the hillside—ascending still when it seemed like gravity should have kicked in by now—and there was such a feeling of *spirit* that we stood staring. Silent and wide-eyed, we watched as my father's ashes floated out toward the sea and the western horizon of the Pacific, where the sun itself marches toward rest.

꠸

Upon returning home to Washington, I received, through an obscure Web site for family condolences (one that the funeral home set up automatically and which, for a long time, I didn't know existed) a message left by someone I had never known, from Fort Sam Houston:

I am one of the guards at the gates.
I always looked forward to rendering a salute when he came through
the gate.
We all knew him. He will be missed.
V. Leon (San Antonio, Texas)

The gatekeepers.
Those who guard during the long, dark hours of the night.
Dad.

EPILOGUE

Just recently I found out that the long-forgotten project I initiated back in 2008 had been completed. It was an effort to create a cohesive marketing image for Incarnate Word High School in the form of a professionally designed shamrock mascot. I felt overjoyed when I heard the news, believing up until then that the project had gone nowhere.

I thought that it had faded away under the pressure of other concerns; running a private Catholic school is not an easy thing, after all, and the budget wasn't padded, by any stretch of the imagination. But it turned out that my old employer, Post Oak Marketing of Houston, Texas, had managed to finish the project and offer a professional mascot design to Incarnate Word. In a profound quirk of fate—and unbeknownst to me—the mascot project was finished and delivered to Incarnate Word High School at the same time my dad was dying.

The designer did a wonderful job. It simply is what it is. The shamrock: strong enough for a saint, an army—and a father's love.

Amor Meus

CPSIA information can be obtained at www.ICGtesting.com
Printed in the USA
LVOW11s1657200214

374547LV00006B/969/P